PRINT BROKER BLUEPRINT

by

BRETT ADAMS

ISBN: 148237336X
ISBN-13: 978-1482373363

www.PrintBrokerBook.com

THIS BOOK IS DEDICATED TO:

My wife **Melissa**, who has been by my side since we met and has given me more in life than I ever thought possible. I love you.

My son **Sean,** who has taught me patience, unconditional love and understanding.

Our Dog **Leela**, who always has a smiley face, wagging tail and is a main factor in our being active as a family.

A special thanks to **Mike**, who was the inspiration for my becoming a print broker in the first place.

Those we've lost. My Mom - **Lorraine, Cesar, Oscar, Vesper, Mickey, "El Andy"** and **Aimee**.

Table of Contents

Print Broker Blueprint

SECTION I

THE BASICS

Introduction

My name is Brett Adams and I am a very successful print broker.

You should know that I wasn't always a print broker and that I never set out to be one.

It kind of fell into my lap.

I can tell you that for the last 11 years that I have been a print broker my personal income has been over 6 figures each year.

That's nothing to sneeze at.

Printing has given me a great life and to tell you the truth, it has been kind of easy. I didn't say "no work" but at the same time, it hasn't been hard either.

I hope that in these pages you discover for yourself how you too can become a successful print broker and start to transform your life in this business.

You don't need an MBA or any special certifications to figure it out if you follow the formula. Before you know it you may have months that surpass entire year's worth of previous income.

Maybe you already own a business but would like to add complementary income to that business to help it (and you) thrive and realize your dreams.

Imagine what your life can be – and it can be anything you want it to be – when you have the freedom to work when you want, from where you want for as long as you want with no boss to answer to or someone looking over your shoulder.

What will your life look like then?

I can tell you that mine became exactly what I had always dreamed of and you can do the same.

There is a famous quote "*Eighty percent of success is just showing up.*"

By investing in this book you have taken the first step – you *showed up*.

I urge you to absorb the information I give you here about becoming a print broker and hope that you take action on it so you too can be living the life you always dreamed of very soon.

To your unlimited success,

Brett

Brett Adams

"All of the animals except man know that the principal business of life is to enjoy it."

- Samuel Butler

How to use this Book

This book is intended to get you started as a print broker. It is not and cannot be the be-all and end-all of information on the subject.

It is, however, a very good place to begin and get started with your own printing business.

It has everything you need to launch your business and get you on your way to earning your first dollars in printing.

It will put you in position to get started, get customers and make money. There is a quick start guide you can use immediately as well as a resource section on the website for the book. PrintBrokerBook.com/resources

You'll learn things along the way after you have put these steps into action. There will always be more than one way to do things that work.

You'll find your way eventually, until then, use the information provided here to decided on your business structure, get set-up with vendors, organize your game plan for getting customers and plan your financial goals for yourself and for your business.

There's a lot to get into here and it can seem overwhelming at times. This is a business after all. All of the steps are simple and (mostly) sequential. Just take it one step at a time.

I would suggest that you read this book in its entirety first, making notes along the way. Then after you have digested the info, go, implement!

Don't be afraid to get started.

Don't get ready to get ready.

Just begin.

You'll be happy that you did.

I often write "don't panic" or "don't worry", so don't. If you feel overwhelmed just take a deep breath and relax.

In this book you will find references to:

- Stock
- Paper
- Paper stock

These are all interchangeable and used in a variety of ways in our industry.

In printing M=1,000. If you see something written as 1M, 5M, 10M, 25M, etc. it means 1,000, 5,000 and so on.

A note about gender. For the sake of clarity and space "he" and "him", etc. is used throughout this book rather than awkwardly saying "He or She", "Him or Her".

This is the 21st century and that verbiage should not be taken as a slight against women, it's only for convenience.

Put this book on your shelf and refer to it often.

Who This Book Is For

This book is for anyone who wants to own their own business without a lot of start-up costs, long term commitments to expensive office leases or staffing and the headaches that can bring.

Being a print broker and the owner of printing company is a great business to call your own. Especially since you don't need to buy a franchise or any printing equipment.

Today you could easily get started with your computer or even smart phone and only a few hundred dollars for incidentals.

There are few other REAL businesses on Earth that you can own for so little and earn so incredibly well. It really is a life changer in my opinion.

As I've said before, printing has been very good to me and can be as good to you and for you...if not better!

You don't need to have ever been in the graphics arts industry to be successful as a print broker. All you need is the right amount of desire and motivation to succeed.

As with any business there is a specific lingo that is spoken here but the learning curve is small. What you don't specifically learn here you will pick up along the way very quickly and easily. The more important things to know are asterisked in the "Glossary of Printing and Graphics Terms".

Even though it's an industry lingo, remember, (most of) your customers don't speak it either.

And finally, this book is for anyone who truly wants to be free from the insecurity and instability of a job, who wants to be their own boss or supplement their current income as well as provide a great life for themselves and their family.

WHAT IS A PRINT BROKER?

So what, or who, exactly is a print broker? You're probably familiar with stock brokers who sell people investments, insurance brokers who sell all types of insurance from life to home, auto, health and liability and finally, the most recognizable - mortgage brokers.

They each act as middlemen for the investments they are offering, insurance companies they are representing and the banks who are providing people with their mortgages.

Print brokers work in a similar manner. They act as a link between customers who need printing and the companies that actually produce the printed products.

In a nutshell, a print broker is a printing business like any other with the exception of the expensive equipment and maintenance as well as the costly overhead of a large building and employees just to name a few.

You are the owner of "a printing business." You sell printing and other print related business consumables such as:

Printing

- Letterheads
- Envelopes
- Business Forms
- Business Cards
- Flyers
- Brochures
- Mailers

Other consumables include:

Advertising Specialties

- Pens
- Pencils
- Binders
- Koozies
- Coffee Mugs
- Key Chains
- Carabineers
- Flash Lights
- Tape Measures
- Calculators
- Letter Openers, etc.

Clothing

- T-shirts for just about every organization and many individuals
- Embroidered shirts
- Hats

Copies

- Black and white copies
- Color Copies
- Digital Outputs

Look around, just about everywhere you go the employees are wearing a nice shirt with the logo stitched in or at least a t-shirt advertising something.

You get the idea. You probably have dozens of items in your home that has somebody's personal or company name on it. From magnets on your refrigerator, letter opener from your bank, probably every pen in your house has a company's name on it.

If you can put a company name on it there is a buyer for it. It all sounds simple right?

It is! Or, at least it can be.

There are Billions of Dollars spent each year on printing.

Customers come to you with their business or personal printing needs much the same way they would a traditional print shop on the corner or at the strip mall.

Print brokers provide services in their printing business – and make no mistake about it, it is a ***real business*** – that many print shops just can't or won't offer, including their "regular" printing of office and marketing materials

Usually a print shop owner will be too busy running their print shop, managing the press operators (or even operating the press), the billing, advertising, ordering supplies as well as the day to day operations of their business that they are unable to source and profit from these items.

Or they just simply think it's not worth their time.

Boy, are they wrong!

When a print broker finds the product or, more likely, offers a product their customer may be interested in, you are providing them an incredible timesaver as well as profiting handsomely for what may (in some cases) amount to 10 minutes of work.

This is in addition to their regular printing needs of letterheads, envelopes business cards, etc. When you are able to find something that their current printer can't or won't locate – say embroidered baseball hats, guess who has an amazing opportunity to keep them as a customer for their "regular" printing?

A print broker is not a "printing press operator". As I mentioned before, print brokering is a real business and needs to be treated as such. As a print broker you will have a number of printing suppliers and are able to offer a wide range of printing solutions to your customers.

They come to you as if you are the expert because you are the expert. You are the owner of the printing business.

A typical business usually requires a number of items to be printed at any given time. This includes letterheads and envelopes, promotional items, advertising material, flyers, posters, calendars and other branded products.

There are also company newsletters, journals and a host of other products which need to pass through the printer's workshop. This makes the printing industry a multibillion industry.

The industry is so varied and diverse that no one company can possibly serve all customers competitively. Printing companies often outsource one service or another from fellow printers due to lack of capacity, manpower, equipment, scalability or simply being overwhelmed by too many incoming orders.

Example: A simple example is printed labels on a roll. That takes specialized equipment that only the "label printer" has and therefore every print shop their labels to their favorite label printer. Make sense?

Instead of having to visit many commercial printers and engage them face to face with hopes of getting the best deals your customer will learn to rely on you for all of their printing needs as you consistently deliver and make their lives easier.

Print brokers are also experts in the printing industry with knowledge of the nitty-gritty that comes with the job. This is important since not all printers are created equal. Many printers specialize in a particular type of printing and cannot do everything perfectly.

A print broker has many of these specialized printers at the ready to place their order with, satisfy their customers and, most importantly, profit.

How Does a Print Broker Make Money?

How do you make money as a print broker?

First you need to be aware of what the job the customer needs entails, then you can figure out the best ways to make the most out of the job. Often times by shopping it out between various suppliers.

Remember, a print broker is a middleman linking customers to printing businesses. The broker acts as a salesman for their own printing company but does not do the actual printing.

In fact, one of the major benefits about being a print broker is the complete and total lack of overhead. Aside from a phone and computer, you can work as a print broker from your kitchen table or (as I often do) while sitting poolside.

Think about it. An average print shop has multiple, expensive presses and a great deal of other needed equipment to make the shop run.

I won't go into too much detail here but to equip even a small, basic print shop can easily cost over one hundred thousand dollars. And that's just the smaller print shops.

Here's a breakdown

- 1 small 2 color press - $35,000.
- 1 small 1 color press - $25,000.
- 1 small cutter with digital display -$40,000.

This has already added up to $100,000. and that's before any computers, pre & post-press equipment, supplies, maintenance contracts, rents, insurances, etc.

Most medium sized printing companies will have a minimum of a million to several million dollars in equipment. Plus the equipment needs daily, weekly and annual maintenance to remain in good working order. They also have incredibly high repair costs when the machines break down (and they do) as well as periods of down time while the machines are being repaired.

We haven't even touched on staffing costs for the pressman, typesetter/graphic designer, delivery personnel, delivery truck and insurance, etc.

They also have operating expenses including phone, electricity, paper and ink costs, OSHA (Occupational Safety and Health Administration) compliance, workers comp. The list is endless. After all that they have to keep their equipment running constantly to pay for everything.

As a print broker, you're able to utilize all of that expensive equipment and expertise with no worry of equipment failure, employees and their issues or upgrading to the "next generation" of whatever is next on the printing horizon.

Based on that – I can't imagine why anyone would want the headaches of owning that kind of business vs. print brokering.

It's part of the reason why so many printing business owners (who are not brokers – or at least not good ones) work 70 or even 80 hours a week. All of that equipment and overhead is VERY expensive.

By buying the printed products required from these various trade printers and selling them along at a nice profit is how a print broker makes their money.

We have working agreements with a number of printing companies to bring in jobs at discounted rates on credit terms. Just like a real business – because it is. (A recurring theme – I Know)

This is what makes the print brokering business so attractive and lucrative. A regular printing company sales rep is tasked with finding customers and customers who require their particular type of printing their company offers.

If they have a multi-million dollar web press, they need to find companies that want to print large quantities of expensive catalogs. That's it! Do you see how much more difficult that is to do? Have you noticed how many fewer catalogs you get in the mail than only a few years ago?

When your customer needs a catalog, they call you. Then you call the "catalog printer", they do the work and you make a profit.

The same applies if a customer wants a book printed, you know the best source. If they need their packaging to be branded, you know of several specialty printers you can buy it from and sell it for a large profit.

Similarly, if it is a project that requires excellent design and high quality runs; you are aware of graphic designers who specialize in high-end design and the right printers to get the job done.

You can also (and should) mark up the graphic designer's costs as well.

Because you have no limitations as to what you can produce, you have virtually no limits on what you can provide your customers AND make money from.

Not too complicated, right?

As a print broker, you are not tied down to any one type of

print job. You are constantly on the lookout for any type of printing job since you have connections with many different types of printers.

Repeat printing jobs pay incredibly well.

You therefore stand a chance of making good money as a print broker when you find such customers. Even if you charge only a small percentage to the customer, multiplied over several customers, you will still manage to profit nicely from your business.

It's not complicated. In the resource section of the website PrintBrokerBook.com/resources I list some of my favorite vendors whose sole purpose of their business is to sell you printing at a discount so you can sell it a profit.

WHO WOULD USE A PRINT BROKER?

This is one of my favorite topics.

The answer is; any company that needs printing.

I know that sounds too easy but it's the truth.

The majority of customers who use print brokers don't even know they are using them.

Because I choose not to tell my customers, ALL, not some, not a few, not a single one of my customers know that I am a print broker.

Let me repeat that. They do not know. Period!

Why? Aside from the fact that there is no reason to tell them, it's because they don't care to.

They never ask about equipment and capacity, staffing and overnight shifts. They just don't care.

If my customers can obtain quality printed materials from me, with excellent service at a price they are happy with, why would they care? In my experience, they don't.

They care that I am responsive, professional and provide them excellent value.

When you buy milk, you don't ask how much the store is making on the milk or if it is from "their cows." It's understood that they buy it from someone else who bought it from the farmer who cared for, fed and milked the cows.

Do you care what the farmer or the store earns on the milk?

Of course not. Your only concern is that you need milk and (maybe) what it costs.

Most people don't care where the milk comes from, they only care that it is on the shelf when they are at the store and buying milk because they have run out or about to run out.

When you put the milk in your cart, the conversation is over, there is no further analysis to be done. You simply move on to the next item.

Printing is the same way.

We provide the customer EXCELLENT customer service, attention to detail and good communication skills and they are happier then they have ever been with their printer as many printers lack these basic service skills.

Here's a dirty little secret.

Printing is all the same.

Yes, there are specialties and certainly differences in quality and attention to detail but for the most part it's all just **ink on paper.**

It's true. Ink. Paper. Not too complicated is it? Look at ANY printing right now, seriously right now. The business card in your pocket, anything. I'll wait.

What did you see? Paper with ink on it.

The customer only cares about WHIIFM (what's in it for me (them))! If you can provide excellent service, be even somewhat responsive to their needs and requests you have done more than most of the printing companies they have ever tried to work with.

Remember how I mentioned the other printing companies were very busy running their business?

That's to your advantage.

All you have to do is be there, be friendly, deliver on time and you will have earned their trust and business for years and years.

Not to mention their profit.

Most of my customers stay with me for years until they go out of business or I fire them.

Yes, you have to fire the time-sucking, low or no profit customers when needed. I usually cut off the bottom 10% each year. More on this topic in a later chapter.

The point is there are many people who knowingly or un-knowingly use print brokers because it makes their life easy.

Simply provide a quality product, on time and at the right price and you will have more customers than you know what to do with. Notice that I didn't say cheapest (more on pricing later.)

With all that being said, many print brokers are very open in the fact that they are print brokers. There are certain advantages with spelling it out as well as being vague.

I personally prefer being the "owner of a printing business."

You should make your own decision, mine requires less explanation.

WHAT ARE THE BENEFITS OF BEING A PRINT BROKER?

Freedom.

Lifestyle.

Money.

Why did I mention freedom first? Let's face it, this is not a get rich scheme. This is a real business. You know that by now or you would have stopped reading.

Most people are going to work at something. Sitting around being rich with nothing to do often leads to being drunk, addicted or broke.

Sometimes all three!

If you hit the lottery tomorrow, it would probably only be a short period of time until you decided you had to do "something." Hopefully it would be a charitable foundation that you started, or something worthwhile.

Freedom - I can speak to this. In the past 11 years (after I decided to really get serious about this business) I have traveled the world, met new and exciting people and made great friends everywhere.

That's not intended to brag, but it is pretty cool.

Money - It is not intended to be above lifestyle but they all work nicely together. I don't know your situation, you may need money now. I certainly understand if you do. Once you have more coming in than your bills, you will experience (if you haven't before) a certain freedom and lifestyle that the money can bring.

Lifestyle – I decided a long time ago (before I started earning 6 figures) that not working too much was important to me. I wanted to be home at a reasonable time (or even be "off the clock") while working at home*. When I started this business my wife was still working a job and along with her daily commute I wanted to be sure that she could come home and not be a slave to the house. (I didn't want to be one either – cleaning toilets is not a lifestyle)

Enter the cleaning service. If you don't have one, you will soon and I promise you will be much happier – no matter who currently does the cleaning in your house, condo or apartment and certainly regardless of your gender.

Seriously, the money brought the freedom to live the lifestyle I wanted. I mentioned that I have traveled the world. A few years ago my wife and I were able to take our mothers to London, Paris and Rome for 3 weeks. It was a trip of a lifetime for them that cost plenty.

We felt fortunate (still do) to be able to share the wonders of Europe with them. Until the day my mother passed, she never stopped talking about it. (my mother-in-law still does) As my mom became less able to travel we were also able to do other, smaller trips, before she passed.

A Personal Note: My mother passed fairly quickly after learning her cancer had spread and I can't tell you how great it was to be able to take the tremendous amount of time necessary to tend to her and her needs. If I had been working a job I would not have been able to care for her in the end – or, most likely, would have been fired. – After all, there's only so much absence an employer can take.

Finally, as a print broker, your work is virtually cut out for you. The job entails finding customers who require printing.

That sounds like **every business in the world.** I told you it was "not hard."
The benefits are many, limited only by your imagination and desire:

*Working at home can be a blessing or a curse depending if you have the drive and ability to get off the couch and do the work needed to do. I'm not saying you can't slack off, I do, a lot. But you can't do nothing! This is not a get rich quick scheme. This is a real business that you can do and provide very well for you and your family for the rest of your life. If you *can't* work at home, you will need to find yourself an inexpensive office space somewhere!

Can I Really Make Money Being A Print Broker?

If you're considering becoming a print broker, you're probably asking yourself the most important question in any business.

Can I really make money being a print broker?

Absolutely!

Myself, as well as several people I know are living proof of this.

Do you want to know why it's such a great business?

Repeat business!

It's built into practically every job you print. This is not like a restaurant where if they like the food *maybe* they will come back.

At some point your customers will run out of the printed materials you sold them and ***have to order more***. They will re-order their printing with you. If you give them good service and are responsive they have no reason to shop around – it's too much of a hassle.

This means as long as they can reach you when they are ready (or you remind them that they are) you have another order.

Take care of them and they will stay with you for many years.

Remember, as a print broker you provide service, and not necessarily a product. True, the service is tied to a product but you are simply reselling the product. Your first concern is with your customer's needs and how to best serve them.

It does help if you are not afraid of people. You don't have to be the most outgoing "people person", but you can't be so incredibly shy that you can't have a normal conversation with people.

Remember, you are their printer. Or printing business if you prefer. They only care that you do what you say and provide what they need in a timely manner.

You will have numerous "for the trade" sources at your fingertips that you order your customers needs from. You simply buy the printing from them at the trade price and sell it for a retail price.

How much should you mark up your trade prices to retail?

It's up to you.

I often mark up materials over 100% and more.

All you have to do to make money being a print broker is manage these 3, easy to follow, anyone can do it steps:

- "Printing A" comes from your "customer" to you at a price you have given (quoted) them and they are happy with.
- You order "Printing A" from "Supplier B" at a much lower cost than the "customer" agreed to buy it from you.
- **YOU profit the difference!**

With little overhead and expenses you can see how you too can quickly start making large monthly profits in printing.

Here is an example:

A customer wanted to print presentation folders, I had a sample picked up (note: I didn't say "I went to pick it up"), and looked over the specifications of the job.

The folder was a gusseted style (expands to hold more). Being gusseted, this was more material and a larger, more expensive, die (to punch out the shape)

Because they had printed it before I became their printer, I called just to be sure they still needed it produced the same way.

***Note:* Sometimes the customer's needs change and they don't realize it. This is a great opportunity to be recognized for "helping them". This also affords you an opportunity to be paid very well as you are now no longer comparing apples to apples as you'll see below.**

It turns out that they used to send a large package of print outs in this folder as a welcome package but now they only send a few pages and a label.

I mentioned that I would send them the pricing on the appropriate size to hold their material and then asked what they had previously paid for these. They gladly told me they paid $2450. for 1,000 of them.

I pulled out the latest info from one of my folder companies, saw the style and price of the new size was $795. including shipping. I then sent my customer a quote of $1895.

They said, "Ok."

I profited $1100. on this one item alone. Do you want to know the best part? They were thrilled to have saved over

$500. compared to what they had paid for them *several years earlier.*

Are you starting to see the potential here?

A majority of jobs go exactly this way with the customer being happy and you getting paid while someone else does the printing.

If that's not an ultimate lifestyle business, I don't know what is!

WHAT'S MY STORY?

Here's the history on how I got started as a print broker. You don't have to see yourself in this exact scenario, just know that you can do this too.

In 1995 I was working as the manager of a very busy Mail Boxes Etc. (now The UPS Store). You probably know the type if not the actual store.

They rent private mail boxes (PMB's) where you can receive business mail with a "suite number" on it vs. PO BOX 123456, etc. They will also receive deliveries that require signatures like Fedex, UPS, certified mail, couriers, etc.

Additionally you can send and receive faxes there and some even offer live phone answering services. You can basically run an entire business through one of them.

Along with packing and shipping of various goods that people need to ship to each other (think eBay), some photocopy work, they might have a business card book on the counter for people who need a business card but don't have much need for anything else.

Printing is simply an afterthought with these pack and ship stores. Although recently The UPS Store is beginning to advertise printing services more in TV and print.

Don't worry though they're not your competition.

This particular job, and it was only a job, (JOB = **J**ust **O**ver **B**roke) did provide me some experience with the basics of printing, at least in the understanding that all businesses need printing, they used the printing they bought and then they came back for more.

To my absolute luck a print broker (of all things) was operating his business from my store as his mailing address and “suite #”. His name is Mike and, fortunately for me, we became friendly during my time there.

After seeing Mike walking in day after day at 2PM exclaiming how he was done for the day and how he left his home at 11 that morning to get started I slowly started to realize that he may be on to something.

I was 28 years old working long hours and here was this guy, Mike - age 35, definitely living a lifestyle that interested me. After all, I was working 50 hours a week for meager pay.

I’ll admit - I was a little jealous of Mike, in a positive way. (Assuming that’s possible)

Getting to know him I realized that every printing job could be outsourced, after all I began giving Mike my store’s printing jobs that we were getting from customers that we could not handle in house as we only had copiers.

We did this knowing full well he was just sending them to someone else to print and making good money on them!

This was a revelation for me and would change my life forever although I didn’t know it at the time.

I had always wanted to be in some sort of business for myself and truly did believe that by the ripe old age of 28 I would be.

The only problem was I had no money to start one (so I thought). I certainly knew I had no money to buy a business.

Each day Mike would come in and tell me more and more. (Did I tell you I was fortunate to meet him?)

Even with his bravado, my eyes opened to the opportunities right there in my store, I started taking (and suggesting) print jobs from our customers. The bosses were very happy.

As things tend to go sometimes, it turns out we (the bosses and I) began to argue, often. More often than we should. I was discouraged and felt I deserved some recognition as I had "brought" (at least through my initiative) a lot of additional printing revenue into the register.

I later realized that they were about to have a "business divorce" and their day to day dealings with each other were increasingly difficult.

I don't want to say I was a scapegoat (my attitude probably could have been better) but soon after I took in a large, on-going print job of a software manual at a very good price (for our store – especially) but still reasonably priced for the customer, I was unceremoniously fired.

I guess the one (outgoing) boss did not like me telling him that by charging a "good" price we would keep this customer indefinitely, profiting over and over instead of gouging him one time only which was his preference.

This is a recurring theme in packing/shipping and copy shops. They think you'll never be back so they charge the most they can.

Naturally few people do come back for those services.

This was not a good situation for me.

Here I was, fairly new to Miami. I had just met my future wife, Melissa, who was a manager of one of their other stores and had just moved to Miami from an hour away to be closer to her.

All that and . . . *I didn't speak any Spanish!*

I don't know what your thoughts of Miami are but it's not all South Beach and Celebrities. Unlike the song claims "everyone" does <u>not</u> have $100,000. cars!

However, as far as seeking employment a HUGE portion of the population does not speak English.

In order to be hired being bilingual was (almost) an absolute must, especially in a retail management environment where my primary skills were. Don't get me wrong I worked retail but I was good at it. People left my store happy. My staff was friendly and tried hard to please the customers.

Some time seeking employment went by when Melissa, with the blessing of her boss (after his business divorce from his partner) mentioned that she had someone who had a large print job but needed too much assistance as she was the "difficult type" and maybe I should look into it and we could profit from it as well.

Why not? This should be easy I thought. After all, I had become the go-to person in all of my employers UPS Stores when it came to printing.

That was when my life changed.

Before meeting with her I called Mike to pick his brain about his sources, etc.

To my surprise, since we had lost touch a bit in the few months after my firing, he was very gracious in helping me price the requested materials and gave me the names of some of his sources.

In fact, for some reasons I don't understand to this day, Mike was about to open his own print shop and became my main supplier.

It was a ***huge*** success. On that *one print job* I earned

$2468.72. This was 1997, not that long ago, but money did go a little further then. And, to tell the truth, I didn't really do much of anything.

I was hooked and now knew what direction I was headed.

Think about it. I met with the customer to determine her needs, priced it out with my suppliers, added some profit for myself and called her back with the price. I was so new, I didn't even have any printing or business card and couldn't get it together enough to send her a fax that I delivered the quote in person (I still do when the situation requires it.)

This was before email was as ubiquitous as it is now and waaayyy before texting.

She accepted and then I met her again to pick up a deposit check.

Talk about being excited. Here I was, basically unemployable because of the language barrier and had just picked up a deposit check for almost $2500. – 50% of the job cost.

Back then that was a lot of money for me and it could not have come at a better time.

I was hooked and knew this was the business I was looking for.

Let me tell you, there were no guide books when I got started and no real direction anywhere. Even today there is very little information about becoming a print broker, that's why I wrote this book.

Remember this was in 1997, before Google, the internet was not the same as we know it today.

Printing, much less being a print broker, was something my friends and family didn't understand.

Nowadays I just tell people I own a printing business (because I do!)

I was fortunate that I had Mike who had become, and still is, a very close friend to guide me along the way.

Without his help, I wouldn't be where I am today.

I'm not sure if I've thanked him for that lately. If we ever meet, ask me if I have recently thanked Mike as I should more often.

My Success Comes Slowly

After toiling around a bit, I was picking up a few printing jobs here and there the hard way. Namely, knocking on any and every businesses door.

I tried cold calling but it was time consuming and I was busy working "in" my business AND I hate cold calling (still do.)

I was going nowhere fast.

I was being asked to quote jobs left and right from small companies who, even when I was broke, I knew was a complete waste of my time. I would have saved gas money and wear and tear on my car and my psyche by staying home and watching daytime TV.

Fortunately, I also worked for Mike part-time doing his bookkeeping and some (very) light typesetting. We're talking 3 line business cards and letterheads. He was trying to help keep me afloat.

For extra money I would also do odd bindery jobs for him as well as a delivery here and there and anything else I could.

It was win-win, I got to earn some money and he got to save some money.

But it wasn't an income. Yes, my fiancé, Melissa, still had her job and it brought in a good income along with a monthly bonus so we were **J**ust **O**ver **B**roke but not starving.

Our personal life was good, we were happy and in love (still are) but going nowhere. We were living in a decent enough rented townhouse but it had one major drawback. Our bedroom window was on the bus line.

Beginning around 5AM every day the city buses would start running. I don't know exactly how many or where they stopped, I only knew that it was driving me insane and we had to move . . . immediately!

After 4 long years, I couldn't take it anymore. If we made some adjustments, we could afford to move.

Two weeks after I couldn't take the bus line anymore we were fortunate to find a rent-to-own townhouse for only $200. more a month than we were already paying in rent.

I was in heaven. For the next two years, there was no bus noise. Melissa and I managed to get some money together to get married and have our first European trip for our honeymoon.

When we got home from our honeymoon, having spent truly almost every dime we had (we came home with $140. only because I became very ill the last two days of our honeymoon and stayed in the hotel bed), I realized I needed to get serious.

We had one year left to get the $10,000. we needed for a down payment to buy our townhouse.

At the time that was more money than we had ever had. In fact around that time a friend of ours told us she and her husband had managed to save $15,000. and that just seemed completely out of reach to us.

Sure we had just come back from our honeymoon and that cost a bit. But that money we were able to put together with the help of some savings (mostly from bonuses Melissa earned) and wedding gifts. Even then I was fearful that we should be saving that money instead of taking a honeymoon so we could buy our townhouse.

Not having enough money would mean moving again and losing a decent size non-refundable deposit we put down when we moved it – which we borrowed from Melissa's stepfather and slowly paid back.

I knew things could not remain as they had been. There would be no more wedding money to help us stay in our townhouse.

That's when things really took off. I was determined to make it work. And I did.

I devised and implemented a marketing plan, after that things started to improve, fast.

By the time a year had passed, (12 ½ months actually), not only did we have enough to buy our townhouse we had enough to dream about moving into a house that did not have neighbors on the other side of a shared wall.

It was a dream come true and felt better than moving away from the bus line. The house was big and bright and was on a lake. Talk about paradise!

My credit was bad, just like many people living pay check to pay check so we had to put down a large number - $30,000.

I also had to clean up about $10,000. in past judgments and the house we were moving into needed about $10,000. in flooring, painting, maintenance, etc.

Also, our housing expenses had over doubled!

Fortunately, from the time we returned from our honeymoon until the time we moved in to our new house, I managed to sock away $70,000!

Our life was transformed in one year.

It was an unbelievable feeling, one that we'll never forget.

We had built up so much momentum that our entire lives took off. We were able to have no credit card debt. In fact, my credit became phenomenal – from 480 to 750. (It's amazing what paying your bills on time can do for your credit score.)

After that we were able to travel often and have since enjoyed a very good life.

This story is not intended to boast, only to tell you how I managed to transform my life and it was possible only because I became a successful print broker.

You can do this too!

Section II

Getting Started

WHAT DO I NEED TO GET STARTED?

Of everyone who reads this book, a majority of them will do nothing. They'll be happy to have this information on their bookshelf for when they "need it" in the future.

Some will be slow to get started because they fear not having the printing resources even though I provide techniques to find some and provide a few excellent sources on the website for this book PrintBrokerBook.com/resources

Others are worried about trying and failing and therefore won't try at all.

Still more are concerned what their friends and family will say when they start this new venture.

Almost all are worried about needing some "equipment" to get started.

You don't need to worry about any of those things.

What you need most is:

Desire.

Why?

- You have to want to make a better life for you and your family.
- You have to know why you want to make more money in a month than you did the past year. (In some instances)
- You have to know why you want a better life.
- You have to want to never have a boss again.
- You have to be willing to NOT apologize for making the life you have always wanted.

When you know these things, the rest will fall into place.

You may have friends and family that do not want to see you succeed – at least subconsciously.

It's true – that may happen!

But let me tell you this, they will get over it and it will be very clear to you when they do.

It's sort of like when you're driving and about to pass someone who is going slower than you. Now, they're perfectly satisfied with the speed they're going but as soon as they see that you intend to pass them.

What do they do? They speed up! It's a natural instinct.

Now, if you speed up and actually pass them, what happens? They go right back to their normal pace like nothing ever happened.

Your friends and family are the same. They will get used to your new position as a successful business owner and resume their normal lives.

EQUIPMENT NEEDED:

1. A cell phone. - I bet you already own one.
2. An email address – I'll bet you have that too.
3. A computer is helpful but you can get away with using a smart phone if you need to get started. You can always "borrow" a computer for a few minutes if needed. Or go to your local library
4. An ability to source vendors in and out of your area so you can start your business.

Visit PrintBrokerBook.com/resources for some of my favorite resources.

Don't be overwhelmed by the materials presented here, just follow the progression and realize that the best of the best had to practice to get there.

You may stumble from time to time, I know I did, but you can and will succeed if you put forth the effort.

Now, let's get down to business.

TYPES OF ENTITIES

In most cases you will need to form some sort of legal entity for your new printing business so you can accept checks payable to it.

Your customers may like or even love you but, they DO NOT WANT TO MAKE A CHECK TO YOU PERSONALLY. – I know CAPS are supposed to be "shouting". I call it **emphasis**.

Do not try to make this business work by asking them to pay your directly or in cash.

Note: The following is for US based businesses only. For more help on your specific country I recommend this Wikipedia link:

http://en.wikipedia.org/wiki/Types_of_business_entity
or
http://bit.ly/4aPDlI

In the U.S. there are a few different entities you can begin with. - Courtesy of SCORE.

Please note: Remember, I am not an attorney nor accountant and am not providing you with legal advice. It is always advisable to seek proper counsel from a qualified attorney or accountant.

Types of Business Entities:

The structure your business assumes is important in determining your limitations and liabilities. Depending on the type of structure you choose, additional paperwork may be necessary to establish the business in your area.
Your accountant or attorney can help you decide what type of business structure best fits your needs.

Sole Proprietorship

A sole proprietorship is the form of business entity with the least amount of legal formalities. In a proprietorship, the owner assumes sole responsibility for the operations and finances of the business, including profit and loss. In the proprietorship form of business entity, the owner's personal property is tied directly to the business; therefore, the owner assumes unlimited risk of his personal assets.

"C" Corporation

Corporations are a separate entity from its owners. Corporations provide the shareholders with the most protection from liability and responsibility from debts and contracts. Profits for a corporation are taxed at the corporate level when the income is earned and is also taxed at the individual shareholder level.

"S" Corporation

An "S" Corporation is similar to a corporation in that it provides its shareholders with protection from liability. However, unlike a "C" corporation, an "S" corporation is exempt from federal income tax. Instead the taxes are paid solely by the individual shareholders.

General Partnership

General Partnerships require an agreement between two or more individuals or entities to jointly own and operate a business. Profit, loss and managerial duties are shared among the partners, and each partner is personally liable for partnership debts. Partnerships do not pay tax, but must file an informational return, while individual partners report their share of profits and losses on their personal return. Short term partnerships are also known as joint ventures.

Limited Partnership

A limited partnership is a form of business organization that offers some of the partner's limited liability. It consists of a general partner who organizes and manages the partnership and its operations, and limited partners who contribute capital but have limited liability and assume no active role in day-to-day business affairs.

Limited Liability Partnership

LLP's are organized to protect individual partners from personal liability for the negligent acts of other partners or employees not under their direct control. LLP's are not recognized by every state and those that do, sometimes limit LLP's to organizations that provide a professional service, such as medicine or law, for which each partner is licensed. Partners report their share of profits and losses on their personal tax returns. Check with your Secretary of State's office to see if your state recognizes LLP's and if so, which occupations qualify.

Limited Liability Company

A Limited Liability Company (LLC) is a combination of the corporate and partnership forms of business. In an LLC, parties control shares of the company and like corporations, their liability for the operations of the company is determined by their level of investment. However, like partnerships, income tax is not paid at the LLC level, but rather it is "passed through" and taxed at the shareholder level. This somewhat complicated form of business entity should be discussed further with an attorney or accountant to determine if it will fit your needs.

SCORE Note: Each of the above has legal, tax, and practical consequences that require the advice of an attorney and/or CPA. Because of the complexity of these matters, all SCORE customers are advised to seek professional advice.

So after reading all that, where does this leave you?

Aside from certain partnership agreements, the majority of small business fall into these 3 categories:

1.) Sole Proprietorship (a.k.a. - Fictitious Name):

This can be set up very inexpensively by placing a notification ad in your local legal newspaper or local paper. It has to run for a number of days or weeks depending on your area. They can assist you with the local guidelines as well.

PRO of this entity:

- You can call your company anything you want, (like Printing by Brett or Perfect Printing, etc.) you just

place your notification ad as per the guidelines to announce to the world what your intention is.
- When the ads run is complete you can take this info to the bank and open a "business bank account".
- Once you can establish your bank account, you're on your way.

Note: As a sole proprietorship you cannot call you company any of the following: Inc., Incorporated, LLC, etc. or anything like that as using this method you will not legally be those entities. Also, don't name your fictitious named business the same as another business in your area or national brand. You want to stay clear of copyright violations. Don't worry about not having a comma and abbreviation after your business name – nobody cares and will make your check out the same. I rarely receive checks payable to my company that had ", Inc." on it. The bank doesn't seem to care either.

CON of this entity:

- You are legally, personally responsible for all debts, liabilities and responsibilities of your sole proprietorship.
- If you have any assets, they could be at risk and you should probably consider another option.

If you're living day to day or pay check to pay check, you have less to worry about and probably need to save the money needed to establish the other types of legal entities. When your business starts earning and you have something to protect, you can always change then. Just don't forget to do it when business improves.

2.) "C" Corporation

This entity provides the most legal protection. If you have multiple partners this might be the right entity for you.

PRO of this entity:

- As stated above, it is completely separate from its owners.
- It is considered in the eyes of the law as its own being.
- Aside from the rare case of criminal negligence (which won't apply to you as a print broker since you are not making, handling or disposing toxic chemicals) or outright fraud, the company stands on its own.

CON of this entity:

- Double taxation - The company gets taxed on its earnings and then YOU get taxed when you take profit. This is not usually the best option for small business owners.

3.) "S" Corporation

An "S" Corporation is similar to a corporation in that it provides its shareholders with protection from liability. However, unlike a "C" corporation, an "S" corporation is exempt from federal income tax. ***Instead the taxes are paid solely by the individual shareholders.*** (emphasis by me)

You should note that I put the entire explanation from above here again as it is the most popular entity for small businesses and the one I use and recommend.

PRO of this entity:

- It provides shareholders with protection from liability and is considered a separate being as the "C" corporation above.
- The most beneficial part of an "S Corp" is that you are NOT taxed twice.
- Meaning you will be taxed on your profit once.
- This is vital as double taxation can erase your profits and isn't profit why we're in this business?

CON of this entity:

- None: Unless you need a complicated partnership setup, this is the preferred corporate structure for small businesses.

How Do You Go About Setting Up a Corporation?

The easiest way if you need to setup a corporation of any type (except for sole proprietor) is to use a service. This is an inexpensive way to go and is fast and efficient. Visit PrintBrokerBook.com/resources

Attorneys and accountants can also do this for you as well.

WARNING: If you have never used an attorney or accountant, understand that they are in business to make money just like you and can easily cost 5 to 10 times what you'd pay for the exact same corporation via a national service.

You can also Google your state's website and learn how to do it yourself. This is the bare bones, cheapest method, if you can pay just a bit more – use a service that specializes in all things corporate. It's ***much*** easier.

Sales Tax & Licenses

You WILL need an EIN (Employment Identification Number) and a "Sales Tax ID Number" (a.k.a – Sales and Use Tax)

For each entity except for sole proprietor (who does not need a sales tax ID #) you will need and EIN as well as a "Sales Tax ID" number (for collecting and reporting sales tax.

Don't panic, they are easy to apply for and get right away. Most of the corporation companies can help you with this for a modest fee.

If it's modest enough and you can afford it, do it and save yourself some time.

EIN – Employment Identification Number (aka Federal Tax Identification Number or TIN)

The EIN is similar to a social security number for your company. It's simply an ID number that you will need to identify your company for all entities you choose except for sole proprietorship.

You will need this for tax reporting purposes when you file your annual returns as well as opening your company bank account.

Sales and Use Tax Number (aka Sales tax ID)

Your "Sales Tax ID" number allows you to buy merchandise for resale and not pay sales tax on it. However, depending on the merchandise, you will have to collect sales tax from your customer and report it (send it to) your state department of revenue.

You will need this for two reasons. Both are very important but one can land you in jail.

Reason 1:

The state, county and city, etc. all want their money, simple enough. You are charged with collecting the applicable sales tax (if any) when you sell your printing and passing it along to the state.

Filling out the simple worksheet for sales tax is very easy to do. You do not need an accountant or bookkeeper for this step.

WARNING: This is very important – DO NOT, I REPEAT, DO NOT use money you have collected for sales tax, that is supposed to go to the state, for your own personal reasons *no matter what*.

This can be a big deal as your revenue increases if you start missing your payments. The state can and will put you in jail for not paying your sales tax. I know it doesn't sound like a big deal, especially when you're just starting, but commit to forming the correct habit right from the start and save yourself tons of trouble later.

Keep in mind that hiring an attorney to help you fix a mistake will *always* cost more than doing it right the first time.

Reason 2:

When you buy your printed materials from your vendors, you do not want to pay sales tax for them if you don't have to.

Your vendors will need your tax ID number so they don't have to collect taxes from you.

Most of your vendors will not even establish an account for you if you don't have one.

Paying sales tax and not collecting it in return can eat into your profit so don't skip this step. In my county there is a 1% surcharge on top of the 6% sales tax for a total of 7% I would have to pay if I didn't have a sales tax id #.

Do you need a license? And if so, what classification should you be?

In most cases your city and county will probably want you to be licensed, A.K.A. – pay them every year forever. Collecting revenue is the business that they're in. Without it, they cannot provide the services they do.

As I am always interested in doing things correctly I will advise you to contact your local city and county licensing department and get licensed. They are usually fairly inexpensive (under $100. each in many cases)

Having said that, if funds are very tight, I know of many others who have waited until they earned their first few hundred dollars.

I'm not advising you to do this but many people do when they are just starting out.

I did.

I started out as a sole proprietor, with no licenses – then got incorporated then got licensed and there was not harm done. Although I think I did have to pay a minimal charge for not getting my city license earlier.

In most cases a sole proprietorship will not need an EIN. If you are unsure go to PrintBrokerBook.com/resources

---

Note: Local laws and regulations can and will change. Be sure to double check this info as needed.

Here is another great resource:

http://www.sba.gov/content/learn-about-your-state-and-local-tax-obligations

or

http://1.usa.gov/lHC4Ci

YOUR PLACE OF BUSINESS

NOTE: If you already are in business and adding print brokering as a complementary side business, some of this may not apply but don't skip this section.

Should You Work at Home or Rent an Office?

Most print brokers are going to be working from home. This is not a bad thing. Others will choose to lease small offices or a shared office situation.

Personally, I started out at home, then moved to a small office when I got busy and thought I needed to – then got smart and moved back home. It is a personal choice.

I moved back to my home office because I can do the job at home just as well as in an office and found myself going in to my office less time per day and less days a week until finally I would just show up 3 - 4 times a month.

Since I never had any customers visit I didn't really need the space and found myself enjoying my free time more.

As I mentioned earlier - It takes real resolve to work out of the home and some people just find themselves un-motivated when they are home.

Where will your business be located?

The purpose of this chapter is to help you determine your business address. This is crucial as you probably should not list it as your home for many obvious reasons. With Google maps anyone on a whim can decide to see where you are.

I suggest a local pack and ship store that does mailbox rentals like the type of place I worked before I was introduced to print brokering.

Good examples are:

- The UPS Store
- Pakmail
- Postnet
- Postal Annex+
- Parcel Plus
- Independent Mailbox stores
- Some greeting card stores
- Some storage facilities

Things to know about these places are...

The Good

In most cases you can address your box number as Suite. Like so:

Your Printing Company
123 Main Street
Suite 210
Your City, ST ZIP

Some areas may require your box #to be called PMB (Private Mail Box)

Your Printing Company
123 Main Street
PMB 210
Your City, ST ZIP

I'm not a big fan of that. You probably don't want your customers to know that you are using this as your physical address.

I would argue against calling it a "PMB" and still call it suite. Be sure to send yourself some test mail to be sure it arrives before you spend any money on printing with that address.

In a worst case scenario, just leave off the "PMB" & "Suite" and address it like so:

Your Printing Company
123 Main Street ***#210***
Your City, ST ZIP

No one is (probably) going to bother you with that.

If for some reason the closest mail box rental store that you must use is owned by a small minded individual and they insist you need to use "PMB" for your return address. It's unlikely you will ever be questioned by your customers.

Packages

These places will sign for delivery of your business and personal packages. USP, DHL, FEDEX and the various couriers you are going to be using to pick up samples, deposit checks, etc. It's all the same to them. Many will even contact you to let you know that something has come in.

This is important as we're trying to earn you a great living, not have you going all over town doing pickups and deliveries.

Mail

They will receive all of your mail and put it into your box. Many of these locations have 24 hour access so you can get your mail any time.

Many will allow you to call in when you're "expecting" a big check from your customer and tell you who your mail is from.

Other Services

Many of these places do black and white and color copies as well. This is good as they may become your source for wholesale copies and you are going to want to build a good relationship with them.

The Bad

- They sometimes mess up and mis-deliver your mail – Just like the Post Office!
- They sometimes lose your package that they signed for (it's rare but has happened)
- They sometimes go out of business. When this happens it can be very difficult to retrieve your mail (the post office may help a bit but you can find yourself with days of mail locked in their closed storefront)
- In most cases you cannot forward your mail out of their location. This means you will have to notify EVERYONE and give them your new address. When the mail is delivered to them, it's their mail even with your Suite number on it.
- They are people and sometimes people do bad things like steal your magazines or worse. Just like the Post Office.

Even though there are some bad things that can go wrong, for the most part you'll be fine. Just remember they will do a lot for the small amount of rental they charge and remember the Golden Rule.

NOTE: I don't recommend the post office. A PO Box is not an address a local company usually puts on their letterhead. They also will not sign for packages for you unless it was delivered USPS. UPS, FedEx and other courier services cannot be received there for you. This is important to remember.

YOU NEED PRINTING

Hopefully by now, you have picked out a name for your printing company or added it on to your existing business somehow.

You need a business card

Before you can get started, you need to at least have a business card that you can give to people when you meet them.

Design one if you know how, have one designed if you can afford it but get one.

You can also go to your local print shop (hey, you need to start building relationships) or office supply store and get one.

Try to go with the best design your budget can afford right now. (See PrintBrokerBook.com/resources)

If money is tight and you're at an office superstore, simple is best. You're better off going with a card that looks like an attorney than the car wash sample they have in their counter book. No one can argue with simplicity.

Do go with a better quality paper stock (stock) like laid, linen or a good opaque. If you don't know what that is yet there will be sample in the business card book at the office supply store and, *if you're **really** lucky* – the clerk will know how to help you.

Either way, the type of paper stock (stock) will be printed by the samples in the book.

Note: Do not buy a free business card from a company that will print their printing company's name on the back of your printing business card. *(Like Vistaprint.com) as* this will not build confidence in your new business.

Letterheads and Envelopes

You will also need letterhead and envelopes. You should have these designed as well if you can afford it.

These don't have to be overly intricate or ornate. Remember, we're dealing with mostly corporate business owners. A nice, clean logo will look a lot better to business owners and corporations than a "nightclub postcard" look will.

TIP: you can have them designed but save on the printing by using them digitally for emailing quotes, invoices, correspondence, etc. Faxing too.

Email

If your email address has anything vulgar or suggestive, like say "69" in it (you wouldn't believe how often we see this) get a new one. Even if it's clean but says something like **BrettAdams2117@comcast.net**, get a new one.

You can get an "alias" from every email provider, like yahoo, Gmail, etc., and call yourself "**PrinterBrett@YourEmailProvider.com**".

You get the picture.

If those ideas are taken, you can use "the" as a middle name. Like **BrettThePrinter@Gmail.com.**

In fact, Mike is known as Mike the Printer. Not officially of course, but when people are talking about him, that's what they call him.

I know we did at the Mailboxes store.

I'm probably referred to as "Brett the Printer" too. It's good that your customers remember your name. It makes it easier for them to call you if they know your name, doesn't it?

Of course, the best course of action is to get your own domain and website so your email will look like: **Brett@yourprintingcompany.com**.

We have an excellent print broker website available at a modest price. See the resource section of the website for more details. PrintBrokerBook.com/resources

Of course, if money is very tight stick with one of the free options for now.

If you're in an existing business, like graphic design and have a working email setup you can name it **printing@yourgraphicdesignshop.com**, etc.

Enough about email addressing – Just remember keep it neat and clean and something you can live with for years. You don't want to be constantly changing it.

SECTION III

THE NEXT STEP

You Need Customers

The first thing I can tell you about getting customers is . . . it gets easier.

This doesn't mean it's hard but if it was as easy as watching TV everyone would have as many customers as they wanted at any given time.

That's just not the case.

First, you have to let everyone know that you are now offering printing. If you tweet, Facebook, LinkedIn, whatever. Get your message out there.

Now don't get too excited because you have thousands of Facebook friends and Twitter followers. Also, don't be too discouraged if you don't have a Facebook account and have no idea what twitter is.

The truth is, this type of social media won't do much of anything for you. Still, if you have it available, you should use it to get the word out.

The few exceptions to this are people in a complementary business like graphic and web designers, etc. People who may already have a customer base, no matter the size.

The biggest problem most business owners face is themselves. They think because they own a business, people should find them.

That's almost never the case.

I'm certain in a location you pass every single day that at some point this year a you noticed at least one new business had opened.

I'm also certain that this year in a location you pass every single day a "new business" has closed.

Have you ever wondered what happened? I mean, they paid the lease, bought equipment, inventory, furnishings and signs. They hired employees and then closed in just a few months?

They were most likely victim to just assuming people care that you opened a business and would start bringing you money. That and they (probably) had very poor management skills.

It doesn't work that way. You're a consumer and a potential customer. Do you care about every new business you see?

No, they barely register.

Look, we're going after existing businesses. They already buy printing, have printing needs and also have a current printer. In many cases more than one printer.

Now don't let that discourage you. That's the way it works. That's our main customer source.

A company that already buys printing.

You can go after start-ups if you like, they are published in many local newspapers but I don't recommend that method – at least not for long term success.

If you need money (via printing) today, then call those new start-up companies. The owner usually answers the phone himself and does need at least some printing to get started.

They usually don't know what to do for printing and will most likely find themselves in the office supply store trying to create their printed materials on their own.

Or worse.

They may try to buy printing from the (usually) grossly unqualified clerk behind the counter. The type that has to call the manager and what should take them 30 minutes now has been 2 hours.

Again, don't be surprised if you find yourself spending a lot of time with them and making a smallish profit. It's fine to get started but not a good long term solution.

You have to have a plan to locate your prospective customer and let them know you're there.

You have to be consistent and determined.

You have to figure out who might be your best printing customers and pursue them.

This can give you an excellent advantage over your competitors especially if you're familiar with their industry and speak their lingo.

If you're familiar with a particular industry, you may want to consider calling on those businesses first or even exclusively.

SALES AND SELLING

Chris Rock said "Drug dealers don't sell drugs, they OFFER drugs. Drugs sell themselves."

I'm not trying to compare selling printing to selling drugs but if you have never sold before and are terrified of the idea of "asking for the sale", think of yourself as an "order taker."

I'm also not saying there is not any salesmanship involved but, in the beginning, competency is enough to get started.

Phone skills etiquette:

Truthfully, nobody hates speaking on the phone more than me. I can't sit and be on the phone which makes conversations longer than a few moments painful if I'm at my desk referencing a prior order, etc.

But I do live by this mantra and you should too, say it out loud as you read it:

"My phone makes me money!"

Now say it again, (Jerry Maguire Style)

"My phone makes me money!"

This is important to remember because there will be times you feel otherwise but don't avoid the calls. Some people are just going to be the type that call you each time, even though we may not want to talk to them.

Be polite on the phone. Make small talk if possible, most people like that. You'll come across some who don't "do" small talk. They will respect you more for not blathering on and on so get to the point.

Don't be the person who hangs up without saying "goodbye", "take care", "have a great vacation", "weekend", etc.

It's rude and may backfire on you.

GETTING CUSTOMERS

This is it, here's where we finally get the money.

We have to go out and sell printing or at least do something to make them call us so we can sell them printing.

And yes, I did say sell. If you've never sold anything before don't panic.

We all sell each other every day whether you want to believe it or not.

You sell your spouse or friend on where to go to eat, which movie to see, etc.

But it is selling. Some people are afraid of being labeled a salesperson and often a slimy used car salesperson comes to mind.

That's normal. It's just not accurate.

A good, effective salesperson helps the customer get what they want or need.

They need printing, you are not trying to sell them water filters or something else that doesn't match their needs, right?

You are simply helping them get what they need in an effective and professional manner.

Businesses seek out and appreciate professional salespeople/business owners who will suit their needs.

Remember, they are busy. Planning, buying or dealing with the printer is not a productive part of their everyday job.

Yes, they need it. Yes it is essential to their work but unless they are a print buyer or an in house designer who deals exclusively with their printer, they consider it a necessary evil.

You should also know by being an effective and professional salesperson ***you are creating the future you want***. It's not something that can be had in 9 to 5 job or an expensive franchise.

After you have been doing it a short while, it won't feel like selling. It may even feel like simply taking orders. That's when the business becomes fun.

When the re-orders come in (and they will) being an "order taker" can be the fastest most profitable thing you did that day and makes the initial unpleasantness of selling

When your first reorder comes in, say for presentation folders, that may just be the fastest $1100. you ever made. (To reference my earlier example)

Multiply that by many customers reordering every month for a year and you can see how easily your life can change.

The Purpose of a Sale

A famous marketing guru and my mentor, Dan Kennedy says "That we make a sale to gain a customer, not the other way around." This is important to remember as you are going about your business.

I recall early on when we first started to market correctly I was called by a company to do business cards. I was at a point on the success ladder where I would have usually ignored the request as every business needs business cards but many don't need anything else.

Selling only business cards is, in my opinion, not worth your time. There are exceptions of course, but generally it's not worth it unless you can turn it into additional repeat printing.

I couldn't gain much information (other than the number of business cards they wanted along with the type of business they were in) from the suspect on the phone. Their office was far away, off a highway that was always jammed and under construction and their web site told me very little.

There was one thing though. When I asked why she was looking to switch printers (you ***ALWAYS*** have to ask just to hear what they say) she claimed she just took over the marketing position at her "new" place of business.

It turns out she had just been brought in from Tampa as a marketing expert and had no loyalty to their current printer. When they didn't return her call in a timely manner, she decided to look elsewhere and start a relationship from scratch.

Her title of Marketing Director (vs. say receptionist) made me decide to risk my valuable time and pay them a visit. I was sure glad I did. After the initial order of business cards was done and delivered (by me), I poked around and after making small talk, of course, learned there was much more printing to be done.

That year they spent over $20,000. with me and grew slowly each year to almost $50,000. annually. All from listening and asking a few simple questions

Because I listened and understood her situation I gained a valuable customer and a working relationship that lasted when she eventually moved on to another company.

This is a valuable lesson, sometimes you can build the relationship, do great work for the company and when your contact moves on to a new job, you can keep the printing you have been doing and possibly gain the printing of the new company from your contact.

In this case, she went on to work for a credit union and brought me their printing as well. These types of relationships can last for years, are easy to deal with, and the repeat business is (can be/should be) incredibly profitable.

Types of customers

We should all know that there are *Prospects* and *Customers*.

Prospects are people who seem like they would be good customers. You get to know this only after speaking with them and determining if their needs fit your criteria.

Customers are people who actually buy from you.

I once read somewhere (and for the life of me cannot remember who said it) and it has stuck with me to this day that there is a third category.

Suspects are people who you *think* would be good prospects. For example, maybe you have a small mail order business you do printing for a good *Suspect* could be other small mail order businesses.

They would become a prospect only after you got to know and understand their needs.

If they were a mail order business that was mostly online they may not be good prospects and not be worth pursuing which is why they are "*Suspect*".

Because most printing is local, you are going to have to determine who your best *Suspects* and *Prospects* are.

It may take a bit, but once you get that figured out, you'll know who to spend your time focusing on.

How do we find the customers?

I'm going to give you some ideas. They each have pros and cons. Some will work better for you than others, it all depends on you.

No matter which option you start with, and you should do more than one, you must research your prospects. Be sure to learn more about them via:

- Their company website
- Linkedin
- Facebook Fan pages
- Their Twitter feed (don't be surprised if they don't have one)
- Their personal Facebook account. Don't friend them just snoop around for anything that may be public

Stay focused here. Really get to know what they do. When you do speak with them, you will be viewed as competent and informed.

Talk about what interests them. You must know that people love to talk about themselves.

Keep in mind, most of your competitors are too lazy (& dumb) to do this.

Note: Be sure to do your research after you have made an appointment, otherwise you'll end up wasting too much time.

Farming

This is when we go out into the world, pick a location where we suspect business is done and knock on doors. This is an inexpensive method to gaining new customers.

CONS:

- It can be very hard to speak with a decision maker.
- You will find locked doors, unfriendly receptionists and be told to "leave some information" for them that will immediately end up in the trash.
- You may be asked to leave the building (This is not the same as obeying a "No Soliciting" sign.) Those are for other pests, not you.
- You cannot hire someone to do this for you reliably, this has to be done by you, an immediate partner or salesperson. (Hiring and training a salesperson is beyond the scope of this book.)
- You will probably be tired at the end of your farming session.

PROS:

- When you go out to farm, on any given day, you will often leave with printing in your hand. You will undoubtedly be the fortunate printer that day who just so happened to be in an office when they realized they needed printing.
- This is good as (hopefully) you'll leave with a deposit check in hand and feel good about earning some business.
  [A caveat to this is either the customer has no loyalty to their current printer as they use just anyone or (very often) have been serviced so poorly and ignored that they were willing to print with the first person who knocked on their door and smiled.]
- You will still be tired, but you will have earned business that day.

Cold Calling

Cold calling is when we pick up the phone and start dialing potential customers. Usually from a purchased or compiled list or in certain circumstances, from the phone book.

CONS:

- The drawbacks are, it can be very hard to speak with a decision maker. You will find voice mails, unfriendly receptionists and be hung up on. You may also be told to "mail them some information" that when it arrives will immediately end up in the trash as they will have no recollection speaking with you and interest in what you do.
- You will also probably be tired at the end of your cold calling session. Talking on the phone for hours on end can be exhausting

PROS:

- Each hang up, rude receptionist and voice mail gets you closer to a yes. A yes enables you to set an appointment with them to discuss their printing needs.
- When you hear a "yes, come see me" get your butt in their office as quickly as possible. You are about to make a sale.

Just like with farming, they are having a loyalty breakdown. Probably due to being poorly serviced or even just forgotten about.

You will still be tired, talking on the phone for hours on end is exhausting.

You can reliably hire someone to do this part of the job for you.

Don't be the person who forgets to prospect for leads in some way every day or at least at a regular interval that works for you. Too often, we leave to meet the new customer, come back with printing in our hand and get to work on "their stuff" that we forget to work "on" our business.

Google Adwords

Google Adwords can be a great way to get your business online today to advertise your printing company.

If you don't know what paid advertising is, it's a way for you to get your business on the internet where customers can find you. That's assuming you have a website, even a simple one will do. You can use them without a website but it's far less effective.

These are the ads you see on top and the side of your search screen. People have paid to be in these spots.

See the graphic on the next page.

As you can see the boxed areas on the top and bottom are the "paid for" Adwords advertisements.

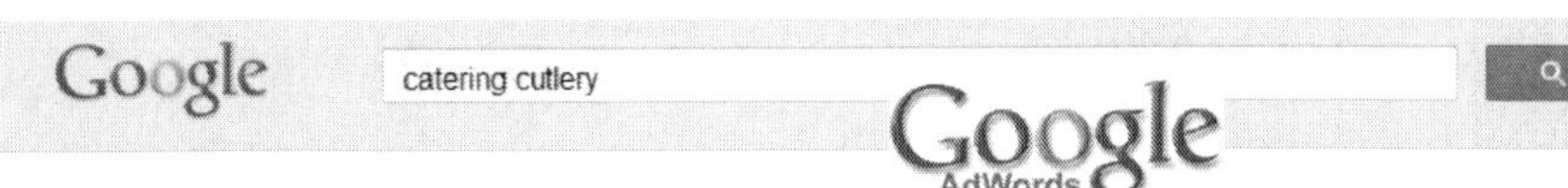

PROS:

- You can be online same day - Even if your business is 1 day old!
- You can be on page one of the search results
- You can (almost always) get started for free with a $100. Google Credit
- In many cases your ad is more “credible” than the #1 “organic” spot

CONS:

- There is a small learning curve for beginners and a larger curve when it comes to advanced strategies
- There can be a lot of competition
- If you're not careful you can find yourself with a large bill for advertising very quickly
- You are basically at the customers whim as all of your competitors are all around you. This type of advertising is similar to being in the yellow pages.

As I mentioned this is a more advanced method that looks easy on the surface but can be difficult to make successful for all the reasons listed above.

It's easier to get noticed in a vacuum with a one to one visit, call or direct mail piece.

There are entire books, course and seminars on how to use Adwords successfully is beyond the scope of this book. However, Google offers very good instruction on getting started.

***Note:* If you search around on the internet you can find a coupon code good for $100. credit for adwords. Also once you establish your business, Google will probably mail you one. Remember with this coupon, you can be online immediately driving traffic to your business. Be sure to take advantage of Google's offer to learn what works and what doesn't on *their* dime.**

Similar to Adwords are MSN advertising for Bing & Yahoo as well as LinkedIn Ads. You should check these out as well once you have a working plan on Google.

Before you email me to tell me how the entire population is on Facebook, it's not the place to get started. Facebook for business can be tricky and a huge time-suck. You want to build you business quickly and effectively so that sooner than later you will start getting reorders. There are specific strategies for using Facebook with your printing business but it is not one I recommend when getting started.

The internet is a place where productivity dies. Don't let this happen to you. Stay aware of what your goals are when you attempt online marketing.

Word of Mouth

Word of mouth advertising, including referrals and recommendations, is the most cost effective (i.e. cheapest) and most prolific source of new customers. We all trust a personal recommendation over any other form of advertising.

PROS:

- The customer comes pre-sold by the person who referred you
- They will generally have a lower resistance to your pricing
- You can build a great business this way

CONS:

- Word of mouth runs both ways. An unhappy customer may tell many friends.
- An unhappy customer is more likely to take to the internet than a happy one and destroy your reputation.

This method takes work, it's not hard but needs be implemented

Word of mouth referrals work great, but you have to ask for them. Without a system in place to get referrals you will get them rarely if ever.

A great rule of thumb is to ask for a referral when the customer thanks you for a good job or something special you did (like catch an embarrassing typo)

Visit PrintBrokerBook.com/bonuses for a Special Report on Referral Based Marketing and more.

Direct Mail

Direct mail is one of the most reliable methods for finding new customers. You create a flyer, brochure, letter, etc. and mail them to your target audience every month or so.

CONS:

- Some direct mail needs to be seen 5 to 7 times or more. This can make for a mailing campaign that may not pay for itself immediately.
- Mailing to a larger number of potential customers every month can add up quickly and look like there is more going out than coming in.
- This method is not recommended if you're just starting out with little to no funds. You can (and should) revisit it later.

PROS:

- It makes the customer contact you which can be a more relaxed method (for you) of dealing with new customers and their requests.
- You get to sell to them in a vacuum. Unlike the yellow pages and the internet, you are not side by side with your competitors.

Because we make a sale to gain a customer, once we determine their lifetime value to us, we can use this more costly (& more effective) method of marketing because the rewards allow us to do so, as opposed to making a sale to profit X number of dollars.

Example - A carpet cleaner using a sale to make money vs. gain a customer:

You might realize every year or so that your carpet needs to be cleaned and call the first carpet cleaner whose ad you come across.

You may have found the carpet cleaner in many different ways. It may have been in the free “PennySaver” type of newspaper that comes weekly to your mailbox, been mailed to you in postcard form, left on your doorknob or they may have even called you and left you a message about the “special” they’re having this week.

Let’s say the carpet cleaning costs $150.

Maybe this carpet cleaner has been mailing to you for 3 years when you finally call them.

Let’s also say that it costs them 40 cents to mail you a postcard every month for 36 months, that totals $14.40.

Now the have to pay for the truck, gas, equipment, soap and chemicals, insurance and one or two employees to come out and actually do the work.

As you know, I'm not a carpet cleaner but would you be surprised if they profited more than $50. to $75. for the owner?

Probably not.

Now, they are happy they get to clean your carpet, pay their people, hopefully profit and move on to the next customer but it's a constant battle for them.

You will probably call from them in 1-2 more years and when you do, they will still only profit about $50.

Their return on their marketing investment is pretty low. It may be enough to keep them in business but probably not enough to ever take a day off, have money for vacations, college funds and retirement.

We have the benefit of knowing that our customers will be printing with us again, next week, next month and for the next several years.

As long as we continue to provide them great service and excellent value, most of our customers will stay for years, some will stay forever.

Not to mention, seeing you in the mail the day after they spoke to you on the phone puts you at the "top of their mind"

It almost doesn't matter what we spend to obtain the customer (within reason) as the lifetime value of our customers are practically infinite.

These methods work

All of these methods will work, making the various costs of acquisition for us negligible. In fact, whenever possible (and it should be a goal) we should be utilizing farming, direct mail, cold calling, Adwords and as many different marketing channels that are effective simultaneously.

Why am I suggesting you do all of these things simultaneously?

Different people, and the companies they work for, will respond differently to each modality. Some may be more visual and happy to see you in person but not be big "readers" and throw away your beautifully designed, expensive mail piece.

Others may have no interest in you showing up at their door while farming but will welcome you with open arms after you have had a good phone conversation.

Remember: All of these methods yield repeat customers and repeat customers are the reason we're in this business.

This doesn't mean you won't still need new customers but, again, you can spend more money to acquire them because of what they mean to your business vs. a "customer" who may just use your service one time and then move on.

There WILL be follow-up

Look, people are busy!

When you first speak with or meet a prospective customer they are in need of printing. Sometimes after you speak or meet with them, you cannot get them back on the phone or get them to respond to your emails.

Unless your breath was particularly bad that day, it's probably not you. It is usually one of three things:

Another printer satisfied their needs before you (you were too slow)

- They stuck with their old printer (for now) because he had their artwork and could do it faster than getting established with you (even though they may hate their current printer)
- They are busy and what was a priority yesterday has become less important because of the emergency they are having today.

Usually, they just haven't had the time to get back to you. Let's face it, you're not friends with them, yet. Returning your call is not a priority for them.

The fact is they will put off ordering printing until they run out or they will just delay their mailing campaign or new brochure until they solve their current crisis. Many customers behave exactly this way so don't be discouraged when you encounter them. At the same time, there are also some that are scheduled, neat and organized – those are a pleasure to deal with and you can get them on the phone.

Follow up, follow up, follow up. Don't harass though, just be consistent in your emails and voice mails.

Do not stalk them and become increasingly frustrated in your tone. They will get spooked and then you're through. You'll have no chance to resurrect that relationship.

Additional Methods of Finding Customers

Use a service like infousa.com or melissadata.com to find companies that fit your criteria.

You want to look for the President ideally. In the target we're looking for, this person is a Bulls-Eye!

Other titles may be:

- Marketing Director (Director of Marketing)
- CFO (Chief Financial Officer)
- CEO (Chief Executive Officer)

I know some of these titles seem like they are too high up the chain to deal with us and in some cases that's true. If that happens, at least you got their attention and they will more than likely bump you down to the person you need to speak to, like the purchasing agent or buyer. The difference is, when the boss says to talk to you, they will take your call and meeting.

However, in the target market we're in some people may give themselves a more upscale title. When dealing with my best customer for the past decade, I deal only with the CEO and CFO. In reality they are the two owners of a 20 person office and come to work in casual clothes every day. So don't pay too much attention to titles.

If you can, I suggest you avoid "buyer" or "purchasing agent" as most of the people in this position are looking at the bottom line. There is seldom loyalty to you and they are constantly seeking new quotes.

Can you find and work well with a buyer or purchasing agent? Yes, but it's a crap shoot.

Don't get me wrong, if you see opportunity, go get it. I have worked well with purchasing agents at a large hospital (but not so large they do their own printing – be sure to avoid these) and was successful through two purchasing agents in a row.

It worked because I was very focused on building these relationships correctly and was able to provide fantastic service that made them stick around.

Like all corporate positions there was turnover and when the third one came in – I was out. She was looking for the bottom line and I was never going to be the cheapest in town. I suggest you don't be the lowest priced printer in town either. You will probably regret it.

An interesting side note to this story is they went out of business shortly after we stopped working together. There were some other signs; such as, incredibly slow payments of 90, then 120 then 150 days that made me wary so I wasn't altogether unhappy.

There is an important lesson to be learned here for all printing businesses: Every printer, if they allow it, will get screwed! Sometimes badly.

If a customer stiffs you for a few hundred dollars at the end of their business life and you profited well from their business, it's not a big deal. In many cases even being stiffed for a few thousand would still have been worthwhile.

But, if you're not paying attention to the average order size and the amount of time it takes the customer to pay, you could easily find yourself with an out of control debt owed to you that will never be repaid.

It's important to be aware of any abnormalities in your customers' receivables and take appropriate action. If for no other reason than to minimize *your* losses.

It's a fact of business life, some businesses will fail. When they do, they will milk every resource dry to "get their next order/customer, etc." and you will be stuck paying for their failure.

The printer is always needed until the end but will never see a dime once the business is on life support. Pay close attention to the bottom line, your receivables and you will be fine. Play hardball when you need to by demanding deposits on new orders, COD with a partial payment on old orders. If you are strong but not too heavy handed you can manage to get most if not all of what is owed to you.

The Lead Criteria *(when sourcing from infousa.com or melissadata.com)*

As I mentioned when you are looking for businesses to call and send direct mail to, the best places to look are:

- InfoUsa.com - (800) 242-5478.
- Melissadata.com - (800) 800- Mail (6245)

You can call them or look online and receive your list of businesses in minutes. With Infousa you can buy as few leads as you like so you don't have to spend a lot to get started.

Note: **I don't recommend buying online the first time out. Utilizing their sales reps costs nothing more than a few extra minutes on the phone and they can provide information and insight that makes a huge difference in the quality of the leads you buy.**

Here's the criteria I use when using these lead sources:

- Not a franchise
- Not a satellite office - unless it's the main US Branch (or similar for other countries) for an international company
- Main Office or Branch or a larger organization
- Annual Revenue of at least $1 Million (depending on your area)
- At least 7 to 10 Employees (depending on your area)
- Marketing Director/CEO/CFO/President/Vice President (First Choice)

- Vice President in charge of Purchasing/Purchasing Agent/Buyer (2nd Choice)

Depending on the size of the company, you may not be able to get in to see the CEO/CFO, you also may not feel comfortable when you are just starting out talking to the executives in these positions. That will pass, I assure you.

As I mentioned, I like to avoid purchasing agents and buyers even though their title say exactly what they do. In my experience they are usually less interested in developing relationships with their vendors and are more interested in getting "competitive quotes". I don't like this. I think it's usually a waste of time but when you're first starting out, you have more time available and it can be a great learning experience.

You may get in with a couple of purchasing agents at some companies. That's how I landed my cash cow hospital I mentioned earlier.

But keep in mind, when their replacement comes in, out you may go. A new broom sweeps clean and they may not want the taint of their predecessors' decisions on them.

So, even though buyers may shop on price, we are not in the business of being the cheapest in town. That's not to say if you're not smart, you still can't price effectively and gain their work, just be cautious.

InfoUsa also has a criteria for amount spent annually on printing that goes up to $25k. They say it's only an estimate but it's a very good place to get started. My personal criteria is, I only want customers who spend at least $50k or more per year working with me. That's not to say that customers who spend less aren't worth it, I just like to have less customers who pay more rather than the other way around.

Remember, these are just guidelines. You will have to start somewhere and start to figure which works best for you or is available in your area. One of the benefits of being a print broker is you're not tied to a physical location. If you live in a small town, your farm area could be two hours away and you might choose to spend only one or two days a month visiting your customers in that area.

Advertising

AD Tips

A famous marketing quote is "Sell the sizzle, not the steak." The sizzle makes them hungry for what you're selling. They can go to any restaurant and get a steak. Whether or not it's good doesn't really seem to matter.

In printing this means brochures of the shop equipment and capacity as well as photos of large presses don't mean anything. The customer doesn't care. Don't show them the same thing they can get anywhere.

Don't copy other peoples advertising, not because it's not a good way to get started, it can be. In fact, there is process known as swipe and deploy that good marketers, when they see good advertising, put in a "swipe file" to reference for later.

The truth is though, most advertising in our industry is so bad that to copy them would only doom you. It's known as marketing incest and you know what happens when incest is afoot, right?

A simple rule of thumb is to talk about benefits to them, not features. Remember this in everything you write (ads and direct mail pieces, etc.) and you will be better than 98% of all the other printers marketing.

When marketing to potential customers, be sure to highlight benefits and not features.

Take a look at the list of features below, taken directly from current industry advertising and marketing materials.

Features include:

- In Business 10 years (most don't care)
- 4 Color Heidelberg (Heidel-who? They truly don't care about the equipment)
- New Digital Cutter (same)
- MAC and PC files (They have one or the other and fully expect you to be able to use it)

Each feature above is a factual statement about the product or service being promoted. Features don't get customers to buy.

Now a benefit answers the question "What's in it for me?" meaning the benefit provides the customer with something of value to them. Get this right and you will succeed in 99% of your marketing.

Benefits include:

- Fast turnaround times/On time delivery
- Award winning customer service
- Professional and courteous (chances are their current printer is not)
- High Quality Printing (goes without saying but it should be said)
- Satisfaction Guaranteed or we'll make it right (few offer anything like this)

Testimonials

You will want to obtain testimonials from any business you can get them from.

Testimonials are the "social proof" that will help people

make a decision on you. All you have to do is ask them to say some nice things about you after you have provided them with great work.

How and when do you ask for a testimonial? The best time to ask them is when they say “Thank you”. That’s it. Say “You’re welcome” and then ask them to say a few kind words for you on their letterhead or email it to you.

TRAINING CUSTOMERS

Don't be shocked by this, you want to - no need to, train them how to do business with you. This is done gently, with respect. Not with a rolled up magazine.

Like most people they want to know how to do things correctly, in this case working with you in a pleasant and efficient manner. If you don't teach them how will they know? Without your guidance they will place orders willy-nilly driving you AND THEMSLEVES crazy in the process.

In fact, as you get to know them, you'll need to explain that every job cannot be a rush. You will have to educate them on how press time is scheduled and that most jobs take 3 - 5 days as an example.

(Press time is scheduled many ways. By day of the week, ink color, paper sizes, length of runs, rush jobs, priority customers, etc.)

Let them know that you can and will pull off the occasional miracle for them but not every week for every item. Let them know that yes, they are valued and appreciated but you have a press schedule and need to fit them in. Because we don't own any equipment as print brokers it's even more true, especially since we don't make the press schedule.

In most cases you cannot simply bump your vendors' jobs that they have scheduled whether you are using a friendly local printer, like my friend Mike or one of the larger trade only printers. Occasionally you can pay for a rush but when it comes down to it, your customer will not want to pay a rush charge each time. This falls under managing their expectations. Printing is not texting or even email so the clearer we make our processes known and understood the simpler our lives will be.

That's what I mean by training.

Your customers understand you're busy just like they are and respect that. No one likes to eat in an empty restaurant, right? You want to see people there and that they are actually cooking your food fresh, not reheated from the last time people came in to eat.

Yes, you are training them to make your life easier but they will get a benefit from it as well.

Here are some a few key training points you may want to incorporate into the fabric of your business from the beginning:

- Not all jobs are rush, the sky can't fall every day, the house is not continuously on fire, etc.
- Try to have them gather orders together and call or email only once or twice a week (especially for ordering business cards)
- If possible, try to only deal with one or two people at the company. The last thing you want is 15 different people with no authority to buy asking you for things. They will burn you out quickly.

I don't recommend you text with your customers unless you're doing an after hours, superhuman, once in a lifetime rush job for them and it's midnight and you don't want to wake their kids. They will want to text you on a whim and get perturbed when you don't text back right away.

Allowing this to happen will make take the freedom out of this business faster than you can blink. In my personal business I work part-time intentionally and texting would kill that.

With email or voice mail, their time expectations are much more manageable. They know that you are often in the field and on the phone. After all, they have seen you in their office and spoken with you on the phone. Emails that take hours to be responded to and getting voice mail is absolutely normal for them. Do not make it easier for them to suck your time. If you teach them that you will reply immediately, they will always expect it and will rob you of the freedom you should have daily to do what you want.

Answering services can be great for this, if you afford a live operator to take your calls and send you a message, do so. If you can't now, try to later.

Note on email & productivity - turn off your push notifications on all your mobile devices and your office computers. A major secret of time management is to check your email when it's convenient for you, respond to the ones that are important, need timely response and trash the junk mail, etc.

Personally, I check my emails twice a day. Rarely will I break this rule unless I'm expecting to hear back on something important. I check it around 11am and 4pm.

No one will be unhappy if their early email comes in before lunch and checking again before the corporate workday ends allows you to be (and seem to be) responsive to them before they leave for the day.

Can you see how freeing that is? This allows me to tend to anything important on a time frame that I choose allowing me to take my wife to lunch, exercise or swim in my pool.

Letting your email control you will destroy our sanity once you get even slightly busy.

Be sure to make use of your junk mail filters and white-list the customers you want to hear from. Be strict here from the beginning and you will have less interruptions and more control over your day.

Firing Customers

I know that the idea of firing a customer when you are first getting started seems ridiculous but I want you to work with people who appreciate you, who will not nickel and dime you and waste your time.

If you start your business off on the right foot, you will avoid the number one trap of ALL BUSINESSES.

What is the #1 trap? It's Parreto's principle - that 20% of your customers will make up 80% of your profit. Conversely, the other 80% of your customers will waste your time, return jobs for no reason and generally make your life hell.

Hey, it's your business. Fire them like they were a bad employee.

I make it a point each year to evaluate my customers, figure you who were the big P.I.T.A.'s (PITA = pain in the a***) and fire them. Usually they are time suckers who give very little work but expect the world. This isn't Disneyworld where everyone is equal and we want to make everyone as happy as possible under any circumstances.

You must retain your sanity.

Here's how the firing conversation sounds.

NOTE - It's best to do this when they are fully paid up or have a very small balance, whatever that number is to you.

"Mr. PITA, I want to thank you for being a customer of ours for X amount of time but at this time we are no longer able to do any work for you. I have arranged to have all of your artwork (if you have any hard copy originals, etc.) delivered to you via courier/UPS/Mail, etc."

Let's be honest, this is a break up. They will probably ask why and you can say that their job no longer fits our working criteria. They may ask what the %&*$ does that mean? I usually respond with, "We feel we can no longer service you in a way that satisfies your needs as well as the needs of our company." It's that simple.

On rare occasions, if you're honest with them, they may start to behave. This is a great time to mention that 15% price increase notification you were just about to mail. Sometimes, they respect being told they are a PITA. They usually know it and may actually respect you more and respect your price increase. If this pushes them into your 20%, great. Again, it's very rare. I've only had 3 in 14 years and I fire the bottom 10%, on average, each year.

The last word on this is something to keep in mind. A $100,000.+ a year customer can actually take up less of your time than someone who spends $1,000. a year.

Where would you rather spend your time? Personally, I would rather have several $100,000.+ customers so I can achieve my income goals, have time to spend with my family, not be stressed out and take many vacations.

Note: If you *know* the customer is going to be a PITA then charge him a 20% PITA fee. This way when he's being one, you can remember that he's paying for the right to do so.

On Giving Gifts (not bribes)

Never give a gift in advance. Find out if gifts are allowed as some companies have a zero tolerance policy on it. Worse than attempting a bribe in this situation would be to insist a customer accept a small token of genuine good will and then they find themselves on the unemployment line.

You can give good gifts like:

- Dinners
- Theater Tickets
- Sporting event tickets
- Local, special event tickets (VIP access to the local food event, etc.)

I have a friend with 6 season tickets to the Miami Dolphins football games and, sometimes he's looking to get rid of some or all of them.

I always buy them even if I can't make it to the game I can give them to one of my customers (or their staff).

Do *you* think free tickets to your local team, even if they "re-gift them" will go a long way in your relationships?

Try it and find out.

You can also donate something good to their office holiday party like a gigantic basket filled with chocolate and goodies (for your best customers) others will get small gifts (food is always appreciated – and easy to shop for, your lower 80% will get cards.

For our best customers, in addition to a nice holiday gift and various perks throughout the year, we have a customer appreciation event where we have a local restaurant cater lunch for them at their office. It's surprisingly affordable and goes a very long way to earning their good will.

I'm certain none of your competitors are doing this.

KEEPING CUSTOMERS

In the beginning after you have met them or taken a phone order (this happens occasionally – I've had $50,000. orders given to me over the phone by someone I never did meet in person) you should deliver the first job.

Usually the first print job is small and you can carry it in your hand. It's small because they want to see if you keep your word. Keep it and you'll be good with them for the next order.

If the first job is too large or heavy to carry (like a case of envelopes or more), visit them the morning of the date of delivery and just bring a sample. While you're there you can drop off the invoice if you like (especially if your first order is COD – more on that later). Obviously if you're picking up a COD check, coordinate with your delivery person/courier, etc. to arrive at the same time or make sure they pick up the check.

While you're there, you can see if they need anything else printed.

You'll be surprised by how often just your presence in their office will remind them of things they need printed and they will give it to you.

Mike was great at this. He would make a delivery and just walk right in to where they kept their printing, see what they were low on, show it to them and ask if they were ready for more. They almost always said yes.

Try to get them to be as comfortable with you as possible so you can walk around the office to the storage closet to see what needs to be reprinted.

Send them Reminders

You will quickly start to see patterns developing in the way your customer orders. This can provide you with excellent opportunity to sell them a larger quantity at a better price for them.

Let's use a case of envelopes as an example - say you see that they order one case (2,500) every month, you might want to point out to them the benefits of ordering a larger quantity say, 2 cases (5,000.)

Why would you do this?

It shows courtesy and respect for your relationship. You're still going to profit almost as much, you're just showing them that you care about making their life easier.

You will also be making your life easier too when you account for invoicing, scheduling of delivery, delivery costs and ordering time, etc. In fact based on these other expenses of time and money *you may actually profit more* by selling them a larger quantity at a lower price per piece less often.

Or you could simply send them a friendly reminder email the 15th of every month that they are probably ready for their envelopes (and whatever else) and would they like you to get started on a re-order.

Few companies do this and I can't explain why.

It is always appreciated.

The place where I get my oil changed sends me a postcard every three months to remind me that it is (probably) about time to get my oil changed. I am not upset about this, I am actually pleased. The truth is I never look at my mileage and wouldn't change my oil until the light came on. This saves me potential damage and allows the oil change place to plan for a reasonable amount of predictable business for any given month. It also keeps me loyal to them.

Your customers are busy and they will put off ordering until they need whatever it is immediately. Remember, you want to simplify ***your life*** by making sure that "every order" is not a rush.

Repeat after me: "It Looks Great!"

These three simple words will save you tons of headaches. You see, we are super critical of every job and worry that our customer won't like it.

At the same time, if you don't let them know in advance "It looks great!" they sometimes think they need to inspect it like Sherlock Holmes. Pointing out any and every insignificant spot that means nothing and has/will have no bearing on their actual happiness with or the effectiveness of the final printed job.

When you call them and say, "I just saw the job and it looks great!" They become relaxed and comfortable in your assessment of the job. They will give it a quick review and move one. You don't have to do this forever, one day they won't even look at it as they trust you and will only call if there is an error.

Now don't call and lie if it looks like crap, call your vendor and have it reprinted. However, if it looks good, it looks good. Sometimes good enough is good enough.

For instance, have you ever seen your skin close up in one of those magnifying mirrors? Doesn't look that good, does it? When you step back and look in a regular mirror, you don't see anything wrong.

Or what about the last time you painted a wall or a room? We spend so much time making every square inch perfect without realizing that most of the wall surface will be covered by furniture, various pictures and artwork making our obsession with the inch we're staring at meaningless.

Ultimately, just know that keeping your customers is fairly easy.

NOTE: If it looks like crap, first call your vendor and ask/demand/beg that they reprint it to your (and their) standards immediately.

Then call or visit your customer and let them know the job did not meet your standards so you're re-running it. It's up to you how much to tell/show them. Believe me, they will appreciate that you're looking out for them and not trying to shove a poor quality job down their throat.

WARNING:

There may be times when it looks like it makes sense to make an investment in a piece of equipment that does something specific and because you are doing this specific thing for your customer seems like a good idea.

Think hard before making this decision. For a few reasons:

- Technology changes – what if a new improved way makes your purchase obsolete sooner than later? (It happens every day)
- What if the customer you are buying the equipment "for" stops printing with you? - You will be stuck with equipment you *will* take a huge loss on.

- If you do buy equipment make sure you have a plan for it to make you money, don't spend a fortune (even a small one) on one customer you're not married to.

Resist the urge to buy equipment for 1 customer - no matter who it is. Things change. Your customer may stop using you or requiring the specific type of output you bought your equipment for.

In the beginning, I was seriously considering buying a rubber stamp making machine and supplies so I could make self-inking rubber stamps for a customer (a large group of mortgage brokers) who was using a ton of them.

I was outsourcing them at a decent profit but saw a huge potential in manufacturing them myself. Thankfully, I wasn't completely convinced in making the investment and as I mulled it around, dragging my feet, things changed.

They upgraded their equipment and network and went virtually paperless. This made their need for rubber stamps obsolete.

Had I made a reckless investment with no "real plan" behind it, I would have lost thousands of dollars and countless hours on that system just to have it go south on me very quickly. That reinforced my opinion of not doing any of the work myself.

<u>*Get in, get out, get your profit*</u> *and enjoy your life* while other people do the laborious work. Follow this motto and you can't lose

One final word of caution, if you print locally with a printer they may see you as an asset (and you are) that can benefit them. They may ask you to buy a share of their company or "merge" your two companies as they see you brining in so many sales.

Keep in mind, the same caution above applies only more so.

Print shops bring large amounts of overhead that have to be met weekly and monthly. You can easily see all of your freedom and profits going down the drain while working twice as hard in the process.

Think long and hard before any type of “merger” with your local print supplier.

PRICING

Remember, for the most part, we are in the customer's office because they are either unhappy or indifferent to their current supplier and are willing to give you a chance for a reason.

Maybe you were on time, polite, actually showed up, etc.

When asked to quote a previously printed job printed by someone else the first thing you should do is ask is what they previously paid for it.

Don't be surprised when they tell you. You'll be amazed how often this simple technique works – asking.

Even if they don't tell you your competitors exact price, they will often give you a price range. You can work with that. Even if they are off or intentionally misleading you, they know you know what it should cost and will only vary it slightly.

Take advantage of the opportunity to shine. In most cases since we don't have the enormous overhead matching a price is very simple and usually still has a great mark-up built in.

Of course, sometimes they won't tell you and you'll have to do your best to be competitive. If your prices come in (what they perceive to be) too high, you may never get them on the phone again.

In a case like this if you have no idea, it's best to present the quote in person to see gauge their reaction.

If the customer seems shocked by the price quote ask them how much they feel you're "off" by as this will give you an idea of what they paid last time then try to get close to that number.

Ask them to give you an opportunity to re-quote it to see where you can reduce costs. Let them know that sometimes the difference in the paper, which press it runs on, etc. can vary the costs quite a bit. Ask them to allow you to re-examine the specs and get right back to them.

Note: This is absolutely true. Paper costs do vary greatly from supplier to supplier, even from customer to customer of the same paper supplier based on a variety of things. Also, various presses may have differently skilled operators and those who have the higher skill set command a higher salary making the cost to print on that press more than another.

Remind them that paper is a commodity like gold and gasoline, and the raw material costs can fluctuate widely.

You can reduce costs by using a less expensive paper. Always ask your vendor to quote your job with multiple stocks - one premium, one standard and one similar that they recommend if they have something in-between.

Often the vendor may have a large quantity of "house stock" that will be perfectly suitable for the job.

Then re-quote the job with your "new" pricing. When time permits, ask for paper samples and present your quotes with their corresponding paper stocks to your customer. If your vendor is not local use Fedex next day or 2 day is usually worth the extra expense.

Most of the time they will see almost no differences in the paper and will take the savings, you can remind them that the difference between the finished jobs is negligible and won't be noticeable.

You should know that I have never had a customer complain after a "re-quote" about the initial quote.

Of course, sometimes you will need to be dead on with their expectations and other times you can be close.

There may even be times you feel it's absolutely necessary to meet their previous price or even come in lower. Yes, I know I encourage top of market pricing but you're in their office anyway and you're trying to gain a long term profitable customer.

Remember, the purpose of a sale is to gain a customer, hopefully a long term profitable one.

What is the right price?

The right price is the price where you are happy to provide the work and make a nice profit and they are happy enough to pay it.

Try not to let any pre-conceived notions on what "you think" "they think" the price should be.

People buy many things at many different price points for many different reasons.

In fact, price is only a factor in around 20% of the decision maker's process *when given nothing else to consider, delivery times, customer service, salesmanship, etc.*

I live by the rule that I can always reduce the price I've quoted but I cannot increase my quoted price after the quote has been presented. Because of this, I choose to always come in on the higher side.

Most of the time, they just say "ok". Those times, especially after spending a lot of time working the quote and other considerations, are the worst.

Are you surprised I said that?

If they say “ok”, “sounds good”, “let’s get started” I know I’ve probably left money on the table.

It’s always better to come in higher and go down, people love discounts so there is no negative connotation with them. Don’t be in a rush to have the lowest price, there is little profit in it (naturally) and you may find yourself eating only once a day.

Fact – Recently the department store Saks, which has premium pricing made more profit per customer than Wal-Mart who is struggling with rising costs and profit margins because they “feel” their customers will leave if they raise their prices. They may be right but which customer would *you* prefer?

This is the area where many people disagree. You will never find the “right answer” but you need to find the “right answer” for you. You will have to experiment with pricing to find your standard.

Some vendors offer a suggested retail price, I have no idea what they base it on, but they try to give you an ample mark-up with it.

Keep in mind, in many cases you can still increase the price a little or a lot with one-time setup fees, plate charges, PMS inks, file manipulation, outputs, etc. There are many of these “standard” extras that you get billed for and can pass along.

Examples of price ranges *(according to an NAPL / NAQP report with over 500 respondents)*

The study found pricing variations as high as *25 – 40% within individual markets*, even small markets.

ITEM: 1M Color Copies – 8.5 x 11, 80# Coated Text

Majority High Price: $489.77
Majority Low Price: $316.73
That's a whopping **$173.04** difference for the exact same job. Do you see why it makes more sense to come in high and then adjust *if necessary*?

Let's look at a few more

ITEM: 5M 1 Color #10-24 White Wove Envelopes

Majority High Price: $355.16
Majority Low Price: $258.62
Difference $ 96.54

ITEM: 1M 4/1 Business cards – 1 Name

Majority High Price: $203.15
Majority Low Price: $114.05
Difference $ 89.10 for this one item that costs between $20-$30.

The numbers can sure add up quick in your favor.

Don't be fearful of high prices.

My wife is a Realtor and it takes just as much effort to sell a $100K house for a commission of $3000. vs. a $500K house for a commission of $15k.

Which product (house) would you rather be paid for? It's a no-brainer.

One final note on price comparison:

Whenever possible, shift your quote from apples to apples to apples to oranges by adding additional elements that make it difficult to compare such as different stocks, larger/smaller runs, add an element such as matching postcard, etc.

You want to show as much value as possible when it's justified for their benefit.

After providing a lot of detail, your customer will not be able to make a side by side comparison (which is what we want) and will wonder why their previous printer never offered them the options you are.

Use any of these techniques and it will pay for this book many times over.

Use them as a rule over the course of your business and watch your bank account swell as you "steal" customer after customer from the "traditional" printers in town.

When all else fails remind them that "The bitter taste of low quality lingers long after the sweet taste of a low price." – This quote has rescued many jobs and customers from the grip of the temporary euphoria of a possible low price.

The truth is, if they are shopping you out, it is often about you and not about price. Figure out where you're deficient with them and correct it.

Discounts & Sales

Yes, print brokers can have sales too. Many times your vendors will offer discounts on certain items you can then offer at a similarly discounted rate.

Other times, you can pre-arrange from your vendors for a discount on order brought in for the month allowing you to offer your customers a discount.

This is especially useful during slow times of the printing year.

Note on sales: – Don't have an "annual" sale. Your customers will learn to look forward to it - like waiting until President's day to buy a mattress or black Friday (cyber Monday) to buy a television, etc.

If you need to boost sales when you are slow, and you will have slow months, usually in the summer, try to be creative.

Once near the end of a slow-ish summer we had a "Back to School Traffic Jam Sale"

The copy included getting ready for back to school and the extra drive/commute times.

It was a huge success and brought in printing that otherwise may have trickled in over the next few months because of the discount. I pre-arranged with Mike (who was also slow) to give me a certain percentage off and passed it along.

Of course 10% off of wholesale is a lot less than 10% off of retail but we managed to still keep our profit margins high. It was win-win for everyone.

Naturally, you don't have to offer a discount to your customer if you are offered or negotiate one from your vendor. You can merely promote those products and keep the extra profit. I usually pass it along though. An unexpected discount is always welcome.

Price increases

You will have to raise your prices from time to time, hopefully not from job to job. Keeping your price on the higher side will enable you to absorb some of the minor price increases that *you* may encounter from job to job.

Your customer wants some sort of consistency. You can comfortably send out a price increase notice every year of around 2-5%. Of course you can make it more but run the risk of your customer abandoning you. I find that 3% is the sweet spot.

Like the frog in the pot – throw him into boiling water and he'll jump out. Slowly raise the temperature on him and you'll have no worries.

Of course, if there is a major change in the market that affects everyone (at least all printers) a simple and honest explanation is best. If the price of gas goes to $8.00 a gallon you can bet your butt that ALL of your prices will go up and you'll have to pass them on accordingly. Things like that happen to them also and they will be disappointed but not necessarily take it out on you.

Dealing with Bottom Feeders

How to handle low priced competition. If you know the answer to this, it just may keep you from having to compete on price and lose business to those that do.

But first, let me state again that we are dealing with businesses here and not low income families trying to stretch their budget. Remember, companies are more apt to pay for the value you bring and not just the cost of the printing.

Still, we all have to deal with it. Your low price competitors will claim that they are selling the same thing you are and to an extent that's true.

But!

Responsiveness, on-time delivery and overall professionalism (including email and phone etiquette, phone manners, coordination, competence, etc.) all factor into "value". What they are offering is, essentially, a watered down version of your services and they are leaving off what it doesn't include (email and phone etiquette, phone manners, coordination, competence, etc.).

They are apples to oranges, not apples to apples.

If you think that your marketplace is always being subjected to a steady stream of new competition that, at some point, your only option is to compete on price, know that there is a better way.

Not long ago I was having a conversation with my one of the groups I coach and I asked them to name a company that they thought might be good to model themselves after.

To my surprise I heard companies like Wal-Mart and Southwest airlines! Don't get me wrong, they are both quality companies that I use when necessary. I just wouldn't recommend modeling your business after them.

Why not? Because they are both "the low price leader" in their respective industries.

This can be an effective strategy, in the short term, if you decide to use it correctly. But there will always be someone who is willing to work harder and longer for less than you. In South Florida there are many skilled people, from a variety of countries, who know how to run a press. Many of them are here to provide a better life for their children, some are undocumented.

It's not unusual to see a pressman working after hours in his garage, next to his trailer or at his storage facility (with a generator) running a job late into the evening because he needs the extra money. Even if it's less than he earns at ANY job during the day.

Think about that, Wal-Mart and Southwest each replaced a large competitor that thought they were competitive on price. Like Sears and K-mart, they may not always be here even though Sears and K-mart were here forever. At some point, today's low priced leader, may be replaced as well.

Think like Walt

If you have to pick a company, why not choose Disney? Disney brings new products to market and price is hardly ever their focus.

Did you know they sell a ball for $200. there? Seriously!

Disney talks about the celebrations, memories and fun. Not price. Apples to oranges. There are countless other parks and fairs that are closer to most people's homes and cost much less, yet the Disney Parks are filled year after year.

So how do you do this?

For one thing, be sure that you and the lowest price guys do not look the same. Or worse yet, they look better than you!

Pay attention to their USP (Unique selling proposition – in fact you should start working on yours immediately). The problem most printers have is they all advertise (when they do at all) that they offer high quality printing and they offer excellent service, etc.

Here's a good test. Get 100 printers and play "Who will win the business" If you ask every printer that offers great printing to step forward, they are all going to step forward. (Unless there is someone with absolutely NO self-esteem)

The same will occur if you ask them if they provide excellent service.

Without ever really knowing what they have done, every one of those printers has made themselves a commodity. Commodities are price based.

As I mentioned earlier, when there is no other option your customer will choose based on price because you haven't given them any reason not to.

When that happens, all bets are off. They will start to ask you price questions and there are many in that 100 who are happy to come in lower.

Why? Mostly because they don't know better or they are desperate. Or maybe they see one of the largest companies in the world and think this is how they should run their business. They're hoping when 100 printers are lined up against the wall someone "might" just ask, "Will the cheapest printer please step forward" and it will be them.

As a print broker, we can't afford to be the cheapest. As a happy, smart business owner, we can't afford the lifestyle we desire trolling the bottom, so put it out of your head.

If a potential customer calls you and asks about your price, you may want to say, "I'd love to give you a price but because there are so many variables in printing I would like to see it in person, is 11 or 2 better for you tomorrow?

Now, you have made an appointment and can go see your suspect/prospect .

If they hem and haw about wanting a fast quote or they are holding a flyer from a print shop that prints their prices on it, I can tell you from experience this customer is 99% not for you.

When you ask them what time tomorrow would be good for them, they will not want you to come – they may even hang up. If you are able to ask another question, ask them what is making them look for another printer and just listen.

If their reason sounds good (not looking for the cheapest price) follow it up with, "How many times a year they reorder that item and do they need you to see any accompanying pieces that go along with that when you stop by tomorrow (or later today)?"

If they mention that their current printer keeps raising their prices, that is different from "looking for the cheapest price" and is a hot lead you want to get in front of immediately. This customer will most likely tell you what they were paying and that they were happy there.

Match it or come in just under and you'll have a customer for a long time.

GETTING PAID & ACCOUNTING

Ok. So now we have talked about getting started:

- Finding customers
- Training customers
- Keeping customers
- Pricing & dealing with bottom feeders

Now it's time to for some basics about getting paid from your customer and paying your vendors. The chapter on vendors is coming up shortly but I wanted to keep this chapter after customers as it seemed a natural progression.

If you currently run, or ever have run your own business there probably will be nothing new here for you

This is not an accounting book by any stretch. It's not even an introduction to accounting and its principles. Accounting is a broad subject and there are many great books and resources out there to teach you more than I can here.

I'm simply going to give you a few basics so you can know what you're talking about when you get orders from your customers and place orders with your vendors.

I'll also touch on credit terms that are universal for customers and vendors.

Deposits

When you're first starting out, you will most likely need at least some money up-front from your customer.

This can be because you need:

- to eat
- to establish the customer's credibility and future credit worthiness
- the printer you're buying your printing from needs a deposit from you
- the printer you're buying your printing from needs a 100% payment

Sometimes it's not reasonable to ask for a deposit and I can tell you that you will know when that time is. Unless it's for a very large first order, which is rare, you'll know not to ask for one.

Otherwise asking for a deposit makes sense *for you*. You are going to have to pay for the printing whether or not your customer ever pays you.

Remember, they are leaving a printer to print with you and there may be a reason other than their current printer was bad, it could be they can't or won't pay them.

A willingness to give you a deposit shows that they actually have at least some money to pay you and there is a good chance they will pay you the balance when the printing is done.

Once they have established themselves as reliable you can move on to discussing payment/credit terms (more on that in this chapter).

Note: Even after a customer has established themselves as being very reliable and on time for years, you can still ask for a deposit for very large orders especially if you do not have good credit or well established credit lines with your vendors.

I don't ask for a deposit with my very good customers. However, if the order is a large one for advertising specialties (or something similar) where the margins are much slimmer, I might. Use your discretion as asking for a deposit can put off your customer.

Factoring

Factoring is when you sell your receivables (invoices owed to you) to a company that will buy them for a discount usually between 2-10%.

Factoring companies will (usually) base their decision on your customers credit and not yours, thereby freeing up your cash flow and money for deposits with your vendors, etc.

They offer attractive terms for your customer and will handle the collections, etc. Of course, if your customer is late or has a dispute with the quality of the job, etc., certain problems can arise that could damage your relationship with your customer that may be irreparably harmed.

Factoring is an advanced technique that you will probably never use, but it's important to know about it.

Invoices

When you bill your customer, you are not sending them a "bill" (even though you are), you are sending them an invoice. Of course you can call it whatever you want, but on the invoice/bill you send them, it should say "invoice"

Purchase Orders (also known as a P.O.)

Some customers will use what's known as a PO or purchase order. This is an internal accounting record they use when they order from their vendors. It's sort of a reverse invoice that they use to keep their bills organized and insures them against unauthorized purchases as well as double bills, etc.

After you give them a quote, they will issue you a P.O. You will reference this on your invoice that you send them in a small area titled "PO #" or something similar.

Without this number on your invoice, you will have trouble collecting your payments.

Note: While it's a good practice for your customers to use, not all of them will. It's also a good practice for you to use when you order with your vendors however most don't require them. Just keep in mind that some of your vendors will and you'll need to create a corresponding PO#.

What should you use for a PO#? Many printers use the use the date and an abbreviation of their customer's name. Let's say the fictitious Joe's Soda and Bottling Company places an order with you, you might use the Date-JSBC.

Be sure to take a moment and review the PO when it comes in to be certain it is correct.

Terms

Terms or credit terms are what your customers will come to expect, sometimes from the first meeting and you should be prepared for how to handle their requests and what they mean.

You will also be seeing these terms with your vendors and should try to get the best terms possible. (Usually Net 30)

There are many types of credit terms. The most common are:

- COD – Collect on delivery
- Net 30 – This means that the net balance is due within 30 days of invoicing. Also Net 10, 15, 60 or any number of days that makes sense for you and them. Usually it's Net 30.
- 2% Net 10 (or X% NET XX) – This means you can take a discount if you pay within that amount of time.

Here's an example of 2% NET 10. Let's say you owe $3,897. to your vendor (for a job you sold for $8475.) When paying the vendors invoice you would subtract 2% of the total owed. In this example subtract $77.94:

$3,897.

x 2%

$77.94

from the $3,897. and pay them $3,819.06 within the 10 days.

That may not seem like a lot but believe me it can add up quickly. Especially when your orders are for much larger amounts. Let's use a larger example:

$38,970.

x 2%

$779.40

That is a substantial discount for the simple act of paying a little faster.

Billing

The speed in which you do your monthly billing has a direct correlation on how quickly you get paid. While you are small, you should invoice the day their printing is delivered.

They will receive it the next day and realize that you are serious about your billing. Many of their other vendors will be lax about their billing and only send bills once a month. When your customer receives a bill for something that was done 6 weeks ago, psychologically, they feel it's less urgent than the one they received the day after they received their printing.

At a bare minimum you should bill weekly, not monthly. You can bill daily when you are just starting out.

In most cases, you will have to wait until you deliver their entire order as long as it will be completed around the same time to send them their invoice.

In some cases where there is a portion of their order that takes longer, go ahead and bill for what you have already delivered. Just to be safe, I would mark it right on the invoice as a "partial" invoice with the "item" that will be coming next week notated.

A benefit of your customer using a PO is it makes partial billing much easier as you are merely referencing the PO they sent you.

Collections

At some point you will have to make a collection call but it is less likely to happen when you are up on your billing and have a good relationship with the people in the office as I touched on earlier.

Beware, these people you have built a relationship with may have a story and/or an excuse. If you take one thing with you from this book, let it be this:

I mentioned this earlier but it's worth repeating. The printer always gets it in the end if you're not careful. Do not allow your customer who is further and further behind on their payments to order more printing. You are throwing money into the toilet.

A failing business will exhaust all of their available credit in an effort to save themselves. Rarely does this work, companies fail for many reasons and it's incredibly unlikely that a few more thousand brochures are going to solve their problem.

Be diligent and you will minimize your losses in ways your competitors won't.

It's similar to this saying in technology about backing up your hard drive:

"It's not *if* your hard drive will fail, it's *when*!"

Over/Under (aka: overs, +/-)

If you see +/- 10%, that means you may receive a quantity of up to 10% more or 10% less than your original order. This is very important to see, understand and pass on to your customer.

In a custom printed area such as binders, pens, etc. Your vendor has the right, with no repercussions from you to sell you all that they produce up to or less than that number, in this case 10%.

So if your order is for 5,000 widgets at $1.00 each, know that you can and usually will receive closer to 5,500 widgets that you will be responsible paying for. Of course, sometimes they are "under" by 500 and deliver 4500. Usually it's over.

If you have not put the same on your quote AND explained it

them in case they don't know it (training – for now and future orders) they may balk when you present them with a bill for 500 additional items at $2.00 each adding an extra $1,000. to their bill (your $1.00 cost and your $1.00 mark up)

Obviously, it's better for us and sometimes there is more profit on the "overs" than there is in the printing. Remember, you may also receive up to 500 pieces less and they will be under no contractual obligation to produce more for you.

Here's an example of what I mean:

I produce printed instruction "how-to" books for a company writes and sells them retail. This is an example of doing some low profit work to get more of their high profit work.

As they have a fixed sales price we work hard together to keep their price low.

This can make for a low profit, high risk order . . . or does it?

I print the books and bill them around $4.00 each. My cost is around $3.25 each. They order 500 each time and usually about 4 books per order.

As you can see, this is not a "charge whatever you want" scenario. It costs me $6,500. to profit around $1500. Now that might sound good, but there is a lot of work to be done on them (at least more than I usually like to do) and, ultimately I am risking $6500. on the job *each time* to profit around $1500.

These are not numbers that make me happy but, as I mentioned before, we handle this product to get their higher profit work.

HOWEVER, because I have let them know that it will be +/- 20% meaning they may receive up to 20% more, usually around 600 my profit goes up considerably.

How? My vendor pricing has 20% overs built in to the price I pay.

For my $6500. in costs, I have printed 650 of these items. 650 of each page and each cover. Yes, some get lost in the bindery process but I often get quantities back in the high 590's or low 600's.

For our purposes, we'll call it an average of 600 - yielding 100 overs.

Let's do the math: 4 books x 100 overs = 400 at an invoiced price of $4.00 each means for the exact same order, I am able to collect and *extra $1600.* on this job. And it's built in to my costs.

That doubles the profit on the job just by using this technique.

This is a powerful strategy that you should use and keep in mind when you're negotiating prices with your customers and vendors.

ACCOUNTING

At some point you are going to have to do some basic accounting.

I recommend using a bookkeeper but the truth is, at the beginning, you won't have enough volume to hire one.

I would pick up a copy of QuickBooks (or some similar accounting book) and follow their simple set-up guide and learn a bit about bookkeeping.

You can get a Free 30 Day trial here:
PrintBrokerBook.com/resources

You don't have to know a lot about accounting to get your invoices set-up. Your accountant can do it for you.

Of course, you can also use a simple green ledger book and have a bookkeeper update/enter it into QuickBooks (or something similar) when you're ready.

Very Important:

You must, **MUST!** reconcile your checking account every month. Not doing so will create an overwhelming amount of issues come tax time and will take much longer than if you do it monthly.

Reconciliation of a moderate business can take you (or your bookkeeper) as little as 10 minutes monthly.

Skip this at your own peril!

MANAGING YOURSELF

This chapter is the tough love section. Some reading this may not need the advice here, many will. This may seem a little harsh. If you feel I'm directing this at you. Remember, I didn't write this with you in mind, but if you see yourself here, you may want to pay close attention.

Relationships

It's all about relationships. You don't have to pretend to be their best friend (and shouldn't try to fake it) but you should make it a point to be personable.

- Make eye contact and smile
- Dress well
- Be friendly (say hi to people you pass in the building on the way to see your contact)

Be especially nice to the reception/front desk/phone person, etc. Remember, you're a guest there. You might be annoyed having driven to their office in traffic and are frustrated and/or peeved at not being given the attention you feel you deserve.

Deal with it.

They are friendly with everyone who works there. They have co-worker friends in common, they go to lunch together and do Secret Santa at Christmas.

If you are not nice to them, you will find yourself being replaced and some other printer getting your money.

That's not speculation – it's a fact.

Waiting

You may have to wait for your customer to be ready to see you. Be gracious. Again, this is not your personal life.

When you are there, you have nothing else to do that is more important.

Unless you're late for another appointment, and it's directly related to the tardiness of your customer, use your time wisely.

Schedule your time properly by allotting for unforeseen events that pop up.

Things like:

- Meeting more people (co-workers) in the building.
- Listening to stories of the kids/grandkids/pets, etc.
- Traffic jams.

I never visit more than 2 businesses in a day and am ready for anything that comes my way.

Your Phone

No one will blink if, while waiting in the reception area, you're checking email on your phone.

Obviously, don't play any games that make noise (solitaire is probably ok – just make sure there are no mirrors behind you) and don't use headphones while waiting – no matter what.

And definitely – do not visit any website you would not happily visit with your mom sitting next to you.

Transportation

In some industries it matters quite a bit what kind of car you drive. Fortunately, as a print broker, it rarely matters what kind of care you drive, if any.

However, if you drive a real clunker try to park a distance away from any windows if possible.

Seriously.

It's one thing to be conservative and drive an older car with many miles on it because you're frugal and would rather spend, save or invest your money elsewhere, it's another thing entirely if you have mismatched paint, doors, etc.

If you have a car like this I recommend using Google Earth to locate the position of your prospects windows in their office building and then park on the other side. You can always park and walk a block or two as well.

Email Etiquette

Your emails should be like writing a letter to a friend – not necessarily long but should retain this basic format.

Hi Mike,

I hope you had a great weekend.

Attached is your revised proof for your presentation folders.

As we discussed, we changed the website domain extension from ".net" to ".com" as you requested.

Please review it at your convenience and let me know if you have any more questions about it. Otherwise, please let me know it's ready to go to press.

Thank you,

Brett

That is simple and professional.

Don't send an email like this one:

See attached.

Thanks

Email Signature

Take the extra 30 seconds to compose your messages even if they respond to you with one word "grunts". You have to be professional at all times, they don't.

A quick note on email signatures: Soon after meeting you they know who you are and don't necessarily need to be reminded of your website, email, phone, fax, Twitter, Facebook, Skype, etc.

You should just sign off as your name as you are building a relationship. If there is something you're promoting, do it in a separate email or mail piece with all of the details there.

Please - do not use text messaging abbreviations such as ty, yw, rotfl and especially LMFAO – if they don't know what this means they will find it on Google and you will seem unprofessional or worse.

Also, use LOL and emoticons at your discretion. It's best if they use a smiley ☺ first before you use one.

SPECIAL NOTE ABOUT EMAIL COMMUNICATIONS

A recent study was done on email tone and this is what was discovered:

- Friendly sound neutral
- Neutral sounds angry
- Angry sounds nuclear

Choose your words carefully as your recipient cannot hear the tone of your voice or see your body language. This can easily become an issue that needs to be resolved in person with apologies so always keep it *extra* friendly.

Phone Etiquette

When you are speaking on the phone try to smile. A smile comes through in your tone. Try it for yourself.

Unless it's urgent, if you can't have a professional conversation, let the call go to voice mail. Don't use the phone while:

- Eating
- Driving (if you can help it)
- In noisy areas (subway, mall etc.)
- While you're at a sporting event in the middle of the day
- While you're in a bathroom
- After you have had a few drinks – This one goes for email as well. You will not sound the same after drinking either on the phone or in email so let it go until the next day.

Personal Appearance – Hygiene – Dress, etc.

Some thoughts on appearance:

This is not a personal attack on your or your identity. I don't care if you are pierced in a hundred places, have a Mike Tyson facial tattoo and have a Mohawk.

This is about reality!

The reality that business has a dress code (mostly). There are exceptions to the rule – cool start-up companies with surfer dudes in jeans, Billabong shirts and Vans or coffee drinking, red bull swilling programmers with soul patches and questionable hygiene from marathon programming sessions.

A lot of these types sleep on the floor under their desk. If you happen to hit upon these cool companies, great, but YOU still need to be professional.

Your personal time is for you, your business time is for business and making money.

Your style of dress should be:

- Slacks/skirt
- Button down shirt or blouse
- Shoes that are clean and occasionally polished.

You do not have to wear a suit unless you want to or think the occasion calls for it.

Alternatively, you can wear a polo style collared short sleeved shirt with your logo embroidered on it with slacks and shoes. People who work in offices often wear these shirts as do many of the companies they frequent. They will not be surprised or upset in any way to see you in one of these.

I suggest buying at least 5 of these types of shirts at a time so you never have to worry about having a clean one on hand.

If you have a great sense of fashion, go with it. There's nothing wrong with fashionable, eclectic and maybe even kooky. The guidelines above are for people who need help in that area, like myself.

ORGANIZATION

If you're like me, very unorganized and keep a messy desk, be careful. The messier you are the more you will slow yourself down. Don't forget we are in this business to live a great life and have some freedom.

If your organizational skills (or lack thereof) contribute to wasting just 10 minutes a day that can really add up.

- Almost one hour a week
- Over 4 hours each month
- And over 48 hours a year – That's a full work week for some people!

You have to fight yourself and try to keep your customer files organized. If you are prone to using "a million" post-it notes everywhere, try this instead.

Get a spiral notebook and make all of your notes in it. I mean all of the, business, personal, doodles – what have you.

Each day draw a line on the page where you finished your notes the day before then write today's day and date below that line and begin today's notes. Tomorrow repeat the process.

When the notebook is done, write the "from and to" dates on the cover and keep it somewhere you will be able to locate in the event you need something.

If you stay faithful to this method, you will always be able to fairly quickly find anything you're looking for.

NOTE: DO not use more than one notebook - it defeats the purpose.

I discovered this through trial and error and then one day I was listening to a story George Ross of TV's apprentice (Donald Trump's show) talk about someone had told him to do the same thing and he dismissed the idea. He just thought it was unnecessary.

Then when he met Donald Trump in his office, what did he see on his desk? A spiral binder set-up exactly the same way.

You may or may not like Donald Trump, but you have to admit he's a busy man with a lot going on at the same time. If a billionaire recommends you do something, it's probably a good idea to do it.

To-Do Lists

I am a big fan of lists to help keep me organized and on track.

For a Special Report regarding *10 Mistakes You're (Probably) Making With Your To-Do List*

PrintBrokerBook.com/bonuses

SECTION IV

VENDORS

DEALING WITH VENDORS

Unless you find yourself a local printer who you are friendly with, like I was able to, many of your vendors will print exclusively for the trade. This can be of tremendous benefit for you.

Trade Only Vendors

Pros:

- They have a system in place and don't need to be "trained" to do business with you.
- They have a streamlined ordering and production process making your life easier.
- Many of them allow ordering and re-ordering online with email confirmation of your order making re-orders take mere seconds.
- They work exclusively for the trade and will not work with your customer under any circumstances (in the unlikely event your customer discovers who your vendors are in the first place)
- Trade vendors have simple to understand pricing and do not change their prices "on a whim"
- They will drop-ship to your customer with your business name in the return address position

Cons:

- Super-rush jobs may be harder to get done
- Most of them will not be in your location and shipping costs can add up
- Getting credit terms (net 30) with them can be a bit of challenge (especially if your credit is a little ugly)

Local Vendors

Pros

- Can help you in a more personal manner
- Can pull of the occasional "Gotta have it now!" printing miracle
- No shipping costs
- After they get to know you a bit will probably work with you on a "pay me when you get paid" type of credit regardless of your personal credit history

Cons

- Usually have no method for simple consistent ordering and reordering
- May take imperfections and requests to reprint more personally than a traditional trade vendor. If he's a small business those costs come out of his bottom line
- You will have to be more organized as your only reference for reordering may be an invoice number which may not be referenced to the previous job specs – essentially making each reorder (almost) a "new" print job
- Are more affected by the fluctuation in paper and supply prices
- There can be staffing concerns
- Your customer may learn about them and try to print directly with them instead of you.
- He may decide to print for your customer instead of you
- You will need to "train" him and his employees to your style of doing business that may irk him
- Will **ALWAYS** put his printing first

Overall trade printers are generally larger, better organized and pay attention to quality and detail.

There is a chain of command in the event of a printing mishap and they have the staff in place to accommodate you quickly if they screw up.

In addition they are extremely interested in keeping you as a customer and are not tied in to a "profit & loss" of any one particular job. If you're unhappy, in most cases they will work hard to make it right even if it's your first order.

In fact, off the top of my head, DFS (see resources) offers a no-questions asked money back guarantee whether it's their fault or yours.

I have used both with a heavier emphasis on local printing for the majority of my printing of the last 15 years. However, if I were starting over again, for all of the reasons listed above, I would work mostly trade.

In my particular case, I was fortunate that at the exact same time (literally within 2 weeks) I wanted to become a print broker Mike, for some reason, decided it was time for him to open a small print shop and became my main printing supplier.

Mike owning a print shop also gave me a first-hand look into the "print shop" business and cemented my decision to be a print broker.

This worked in my favor as the internet was still in its infancy and it was harder to locate trade sources. Mike had been a print broker for years and was a big help along the way.

The fact that we were friendly before our actual "working" relationship began was a happy bonus. Also, he didn't look down on me as a "print broker" as many local printers and various people in the industry do – even though every printer brokers (outsources) at least one thing.

Vendor pricing can and will be different from vendor to vendor for the same job. They will almost always match a price as well.

Shipping can also be very costly on some jobs so keep that in mind when ordering. My business is in Florida so it is much less expensive for me to source larger items that ship from the South East area whenever possible.

There may be exceptions but 2 pallets on a truck from Oregon will cost a lot more than from Georgia.

Be cordial, they are people to. As corny as it sounds, ask them about the weather especially if they live in a different climate than you do. Then commiserate with them in a friendly way. They all ask me how the weather is where I live. I tell them it's great, hot and sunny as always.

Things to be aware of when using local printers:

- Bad printing
- Price variations
- "Stealing" customers

Vendors & Credit

Some may ask to run your credit. This doesn't mean if you have bad credit you can't do business with them, it just means you may need to pay COD. That's life, get over it. Start earning and paying your bills timely and your credit will be excellent in no time.

Things most common things that can go wrong: (in no means a complete list)

- Wrong paper
- Wrong ink
- Wrong/bad fold
- Wrong/bad trim
- Poor quality
- Late (beyond deadline)

An important note about freight shipping and charges:

Be careful when you are ordering a large quantity of anything that is not arriving via UPS or FedEx.

Most companies ship “FOB” – Free on Board (also commonly referred to as freight on board). It often appears as like “FOB Factory” or “FOB Origin” too.

Basically, this means that they are no longer responsible for the shipment once it leaves their production facility.

They will arrange to have the product loaded on a truck and delivered to you – you pay the shipping unless spelled out in advance.

One thing to look out for when you see this is:

The product is NOT insured by them or the carrier.

This means that you can have several thousands of dollars of product on a truck somewhere, subject to the forces of nature and incompetence and YOU are responsible.

In this case, you will want to insure it in some form or

fashion, usually via the carrier (trucking line).

Ask for details about this, it's very important. (Water, snow and other damage does happen to shipments in transit. You want to be certain that you do not have to pay for this job twice!)

The product does NOT include "inside delivery".

If you are fortunate that the customer has a loading dock and forklift, you are ok. Otherwise, in most cases, someone has to be there to unload or at the least bring it inside the customer's building.

You do not want to be the person who does this. Unloading several pallets of product into a small freight elevator (or worse – no elevator) will ruin your day.

Be sure to inquire about insurance and inside delivery when you are getting the quote from your vendor to pass along the charges.

Any competitors quote will have shipping (including inside delivery) broken out as a separate item. It's important that you do the same in order to keep the "apples to apples" comparison neutral.

"FOB Destination" means the Seller (your vendor) bears the responsibility of the delivery to your destinations door. This usually does not include "inside delivery" so be sure to have an understanding of where these materials are being delivered.

This is essentially contract law and is beyond the scope of this book. Reputable companies should help you with this when you ask.

Now that you have this knowledge – ASK! It's crucial.

ADVERTISING SPECIALTIES

Understanding Catalog Pricing

Often times your customer will want specialty items such as pens, shirts, etc. that may come in the form of a printed catalog from your vendor. In most cases the supplier has printed the pricing right in the catalog.

To more clearly explain it, I have asked my friend, former writer for *Quick Printing Magazine (among many other things),* Cy Stapleton to allow me to reprint one of his articles on the subject. Aside from a slight updating, there was no sense in re-writing this as it is well explained.

A tutorial on how to get into the advertising specialty business as an outstanding profit center.

by Cy Stapleton (c) (slightly updated by me)

Advertising specialties can be a major profit center for the small to medium-size printer. Many printers I have spoken to indicate an interest in ad specialties but are under the mistaken opinion that they have to belong to some kind of clique, association, or whatever to get started.

Nothing is further from the truth. There are major players who have virtually controlled the industry for years, but we will address that later. Like the printing industry, there are some things you need to know and some terms you must learn, but it's not that difficult. We will cover some of these things later in this chapter.

You already have the basics a place of business, a telephone, a resale certificate, and a bunch of printing customers who are prospects. It will take a little work on your part, but I can guarantee you that work will be rewarding.

If you want to get your feet wet, you can get started immediately by working with one of the trade journal advertisers who are already in the business and will do the legwork, find what you are looking for, and enter your order for you, allowing you a very nice margin of profit. Just look in the classified section under "Advertising Specialties." Or you can try one of the resources listed at the end of this chapter.

I am going to attempt to un-shroud the mystique of the advertising specialty business and give you the basic information to take advantage of this incredible profit center. Ad specialty salespeople are selling printing, so there is no reason you should not consider selling ad specialties.

What I will attempt to cover and the order I intend to cover it in is: "A basic introduction to ad specialties, what they are and how they are used and some resources to get you started" "How to read and understand the hidden codes in catalogs and price sheets "Understanding how to break through the difficult-to-penetrate curtain major players in this industry have created" "How to talk to a manufacturer" "Understanding how the image is put on the item and how it differs from the normal printing methods we are familiar with" "Marketing ideas" "Hitting on new and upcoming products, how they can be used, etc."

The Silent Salesperson

Businesses want their company name in front of their customers and potential customers as much as possible. The use of ad specialties is an excellent method for a company to place its name onto various items which people use every day, thus continually putting their name in front of customers and potential customers. It's almost like having a silent salesperson. I would have a hard time forgetting about the Girl Scouts even if my bride were not the District Chairman. The Girl Scout coffee cup at my desk has been filled literally thousands of times over the years. I would have a hard time forgetting Olmsted Kirk Paper Company. I love that large wall calendar with the big blocks that my salesman, Brian Bennett, gives me each year. Every time I pick up my type size finder, I see the name "Service Engravers." I may have to look at the item to get their address, but when I get a Hotline call from a printer looking for a type size finder I don't have to go to the Hotline database Service Engravers is engraved in my brain. These are all ad specialties.

Ad specialties are also great motivators for salespersons. Giving promotional items leaves the perception that the company is successful and success breeds success. That is why it is so important to know what ad specialties are and how to achieve the most out of using them.

You must show the right products to your customer. You need to find out just what your customer wants to achieve and look for a product that will help him do that. There are so many different products being produced all over the world that there should be no problem in finding the right one for your customer. As an example, if a convenience store wants to push the fact that they sell state lottery tickets, you could suggest an inexpensive ad specialty item with their imprint to pick numbers or another to scratch off their scratch-off tickets. Or if your customer sells computer software, you could suggest a letter opener shaped like a computer diskette.

When I got started in this business in 1959, one of the first things I did was to purchase 1,000 vinyl matchbook covers from Royal Die Cutting and Heat Sealing. I was a "notebook engineer" (loose leaf binder salesman) for the Inter City Manufacturing Company. I wanted a small line of non-competitive products to sell to my customers. A friend suggested ad specialties. The first catalog I received was from Royal and my first order was for my own item a very inexpensive cover for a 20-match matchbook. Smoking was much more prevalent at that time and in the Houston heat, if you put a matchbook in your shirt pocket, shortly it would be so damp the matches wouldn't strike. This inexpensive give-away had my name and phone number printed on it. A potential customer might lose my business card, but they would find some way to get in touch with me if they lost their matchbook cover. Over 30 years later, I still occasionally run into someone who reminds me of that ad specialty item. It was the right product for me an advertising specialty that paid for itself many times over.

Virtually every one of your customers is a prospect for some kind of ad specialty item. You want to be their full-line graphic arts consultant. You want to provide them with their "matchbook cover."

What is an ad specialty?

An ad specialty is any item which has information, logos, etc. printed directly upon it. Ad specialties can be as simple as a scratch pad or as high-tech as a computer. Many manufacturers actually produce ad specialties without realizing that they are doing so.

Ad specialties come in many shapes and sizes, and they range in cost from emery boards that cost a few cents to thousands of dollars for some high end executive gifts. Companies use them to promote themselves and their products, as incentives, for trade show advertising, as general product advertising, and to generate company name recognition.

The item chosen should always fit the occasion in which it is to be presented to prospects and existing customers. A good example of this is an exhibitor at a trade show handing out printed plastic bags. In order to be the most effective with this form of advertising the exhibitor should purchase a larger and higher quality bag. I can't begin to tell you how many trade show attendees have come up to me to ask if I knew where they could get one of those long skinny plastic bags that they could roll up, insert and protect the many posters they collect from exhibitors. Or from exhibitors who want a certain type of bag that they have seen for the next trade show. I sometimes feel I am working more for Komori or Heidelberg or Jack Seimer of Sacs & Boxes.

Questions you need to ask are:

- What image is your customer looking to project?
- What type of budget does she have?
- How many pieces does she need?

Once these questions have been answered, it is much easier to find the product that will meet her requirement and you can show and sell those products.

Estimating advertising specialties is simple. All of your pricing information is generally printed on the price sheet or in the catalog. On any given item, your gross profit can be from 20 to 100 percent or more. The work it takes to process an order is basic, but don't be fooled into not monitoring the status of each order until it is delivered. We will cover that later.

The Advertising Specialty Institute (ASI – ASI #)

I used to operate the free source search service, *Helene's Hotline (before retirement)*, and it was not uncommon for me to receive a fax from a reader who had attempted to contact a source he received from *Hotline* telling me the customer service person (CSR) asked "What is your ASI number?" Never having heard of "ASI," he told the CSR that he had gotten the company's name from *Helene's Hotline.* The CSR would then probably say that she had never heard of *Helene's Hotline,* and if he wasn't a member of ASI she was wasting her time and his.

More often than not the vendors management had indicated that the company was very much interested in attracting new legitimate dealers. The problem is that for years the private company, "Advertising Specialty Institute (ASI)," has maintained such a tight control over the industry that the fact that managements desire to expand their market to other legitimate resellers has not yet reached the customer service level.

Many CSRs are still of the mindset that if you are not a member of ASI you are not in the ad specialty business. Except for the fact that ASI is not a trade association, that is not unlike our Printing Industries Association attempting to dissuade paper houses from selling to any printer who was not a member of PIA. Just keep in mind that even in your own company your janitor or delivery person can say "no!" The printer must understand this mindset or he will have a difficult time overcoming it.

The Advertising Specialty Institute (ASI) is not an association like our Printing Industries Associations but rather a "for- profit" private enterprise. They provide many outstanding services to their "members" (subscribers) but are very protective of their niche. They have a rather substantial membership fee for both vendors and dealers. They attempt to place stumbling blocks in the path of those who want to get involved in the industry.

Just wanting to become a part of the industry is not enough. You must be able to document that you have made purchases from a fairly significant number of their vendor subscribers within the last 90 or so days. It puts you in a "Catch 22" position. Those sales must be from their vendor subscribers to be counted not from among the hundreds of non-subscribing manufacturers. In the most basic terms, think of ASI as a very large printing company who has as captive accounts a couple of thousand customers they print catalogs for and also provides (for a fee) many other services to both those customers and to their customers. Heck of a deal.

ASI assigns each subscriber both vendor and dealer - something that is called an "ASI number." For the printer, that number has little significance. What you are interested in is the contact information for the direct manufacturers, the products those manufacturers produce, and in some cases the manufacturers "line name." Once you have that information, you can contact the manufacturer directly and request a set of his catalogs. There are several sources other than ASI for that information that you will find at the end of this chapter.

Keep in mind that these manufacturers are in the business to sell product. However, they are the epitome of a trade shop. They will not sell directly to the end user. You are exactly what they are looking for in the way of a new dealer. You have a business location, a legitimate resellers number, a sales force (or at least some regular contact with your customers), a large number of existing customers (each of whom is a prospect for ad specialties), and most important, many ad specialty dealers are already selling printing in direct competition with you.

When you contact a manufacturer, you should introduce yourself to the CSR as pleasantly as possible by saying, "I am John Jones of Jones Printing Company and Promotional Products. I have a customer who is interested in 250 of your vinyl key tags, red and imprinted in white with art that I will provide. I do not have a current catalog. Can you please give me a price and turnaround time? Also, can you send me three copies of your current catalog?" The CSR will probably say "That will be $.65 each on an A." (We will cover the discount codes a little later.)

What you have done is, by adding "and Promotional Products," you immediately let the CSR know you are in the business. You have let the CSR know that you have the capability of producing (or obtaining) artwork. You also have let the CSR know you don't have a "current" catalog (not that you don't have any catalog at all.) And, very important, you don't ask what "on an A" means.

If the CSR asks for your ASI number, simply tell them that you are a reseller but are not a member of the Advertising Specialty Institute. If they give you any problem, simply say, "Thank you," and call the next vendor for that product on your list.

I received a *Hotline* inquiry from a printer who was looking for 75,000 wooden nickels. I gave him the name of a vendor who expressed to me at a trade show that his company would love to add printers to their distributor list. The printer contacted the vendor and was told by the CSR that they did not sell to printer's they only sold to ASI members. The printer called me for another potential source, I gave it to him and he got the job. The manufacturer was happy, the printer was happy, the printer's customer was happy, and the first manufacturer called has permanently lost what might well have turned out to be a pretty decent account.

When you deal with ad specialty manufacturers, you must get across to them that you are a reseller and that you have a customer who is looking for their product. You certainly do not want your first contact with the company giving you a tough time to be a product with your company name on it.

You will want to start building a collection of catalogs. I have found the best way to do that is to write a brief boilerplate letter (or email) that contains the following information worded in your own words: You are a small commercial printer and ad specialty dealer and would like a minimum of three sets of their catalogs one for your customer service area, one for your office file and one for your sales staff. You will want to address each letter to the sales contact or "sales manager" of each company. As the catalogs come in, file one copy of each (alphabetically by line name) along with all of the accompanying sales literature and note in your database that you have a catalog on file. Put the second copy in your customer service area. You will then have at least one set remaining that you can let a customer borrow, if necessary.

How to read the discount codes

The manufacturer's price sheets include full color illustrations of each product, the pricing information in various quantities for each product, etc. In the front or back of the catalog you will normally find information such as delivery times, set up charges, etc. These catalogs are for the most part very easy to use and read, and you can show them to your customer. The manufacturers contact information appears nowhere in the catalog. It is identified by a "Line name." The prices shown are all "retail" prices.

Hidden on each page (or in the information section at the front or back of the catalog) you will find a discount code. It will not jump off the page at you, but it is easily found. As an example, let's say you are looking at a ballpoint pen in the "Fun Line" catalog. The price on the catalog sheet is $.37 for 50, $.33 for 100, $.30 for 250, $.28 for 500, $.25 for 1,000 and $.22 for 2,500. In tiny type on the page you see a code that says 2A2BCD. That code means that the first two brackets (50 and 100) take a 50 percent discount, the next two brackets (250 and 500) take a 45 percent discount, the next bracket (1,000) takes a 40 percent discount and the final bracket (2,500) takes a 35 percent discount. You will also need to check the "additional charges" section to see what the discounts on such things as dies, set up charges, custom colors, etc. take.

The discount codes start at A or P with each being 50 percent and decreasing 5 percent with each successive letter. In other words a B is 45 percent, C is 40 percent, D is 35 percent, E is 30 percent, etc.

The chart below should make it more clear:

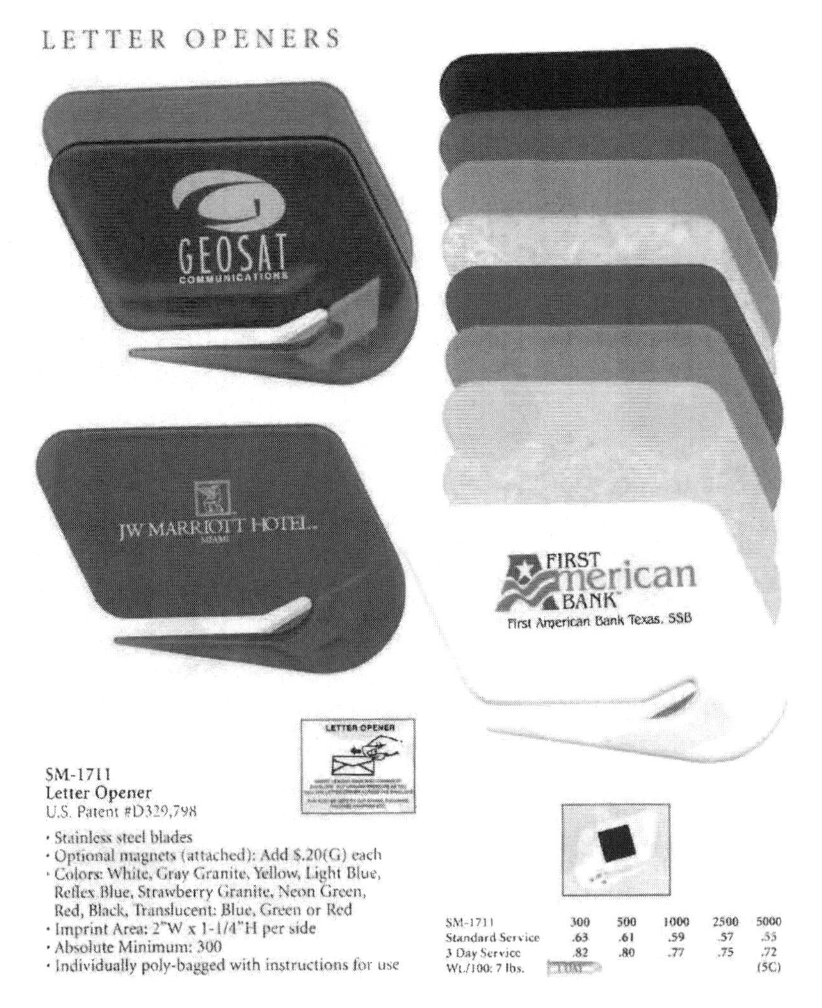

LETTER OPENERS

SM-1711
Letter Opener
U.S. Patent #D329,798

- Stainless steel blades
- Optional magnets (attached): Add $.20(G) each
- Colors: White, Gray Granite, Yellow, Light Blue, Reflex Blue, Strawberry Granite, Neon Green, Red, Black, Translucent: Blue, Green or Red
- Imprint Area: 2"W x 1-1/4"H per side
- Absolute Minimum: 300
- Individually poly-bagged with instructions for use

SM-1711	300	500	1000	2500	5000
Standard Service	.63	.61	.59	.57	.55
3 Day Service	.82	.80	.77	.75	.72
Wt./100: 7 lbs.	1 DAY				(5C)

Set-Up Charge: $50.00(G), $25.00(G) on re-orders. **Additional Color/Location:** SM-1711 & SM-3240: $50.00(G) set-up plus .25(G) per piece run charge per color/side; SM-3236: $50.00(G) set-up plus .35(G) per piece run charge per color/location.

1 DAY Add 20% to 3 day price. (see page 235)

108

The same thing holds for P, Q, R, S, T, etc. (Instead of A, B, C, D, etc.) 50 percent, 45 percent, 40 percent, 35 percent, 30 percent, etc.

When you get an order, you will have to go to your file (or database) to find the contact information for the "Fun Line" is actually ABC Corp. The company contact information will normally appear nowhere on their catalog. This way you can feel comfortable in showing the catalog to your customer.

There are a couple of things that you must keep in mind. Some advertising specialty lines are "franchised" or "restricted." You cannot deal directly with the franchised lines. They only deal through franchised dealers. In the case of companies like Zippo or Cross, you will have to go through one of their franchised dealers. In the case of "restricted" manufacturers, they may or may not sell to you directly. These "franchised" or "authorized" dealers will generally work out a split on the discount with you. Many "restricted" manufacturers will sell to you directly if you approach them properly.

Samples...

Even more than in traditional printing, samples are used to sell. Many manufacturers have elaborate sample cases that beautifully and conveniently display their product line. Others have loose samples. Most have a small fee for their samples. It's very easy to go overboard on ordering samples. Even if you are highly selective in what you order, it will not be long before you will be needing more space to store or display them.

Don't always depend upon your gut feeling as to what will sell. There have been items I felt I could sell to a dozen or more of my customers, but I wasn't able to sell a single one. Other items I would never have considered as being "hot" turned out to be best sellers. Take advantage of your supplier's expertise. Ask them what their hottest products are for certain types of customers and order those.

Practice what you preach. If you are selling ad specialties, you want to have at least one or two with your name on it. Scratch pads are certainly a good choice because you can print them yourself, but also consider something like a nice ballpoint pen, a razor letter opener, a coffee cup, a small desk calendar or a huge wall year-at-a-glance calendar.

Many suppliers have regular specials. They provide you either with the digital files of these specials where you can plug in your name and run however many copies you require, or they will provide a quantity of full color special sheets with your name imprinted on it for a small fee. These make excellent statement stuffers and promotional pieces to include with every order you print.

Just take a look at your customer list. Then take a look through your catalogs. Pick out one or two items you feel would be appropriate for each of a dozen or so of your customers and order samples of those items. When you call on that customer or when he comes into your shop, show him the samples and give him a price on various quantities. I'll bet you will be surprised at the results. When you've gone through that first group, do the same thing for another dozen or so customers.

September or October is a great time to start contacting your hotels, clubs and bars about New Years Eve party favors. Yes, they are considered ad specialties too, and there are big, big profits in these sales. A seriously "physically challenged" friend in Houston sold nothing but New Years Eve party favors and he did it all by phone in October, November and December. Come delivery time he would hire college students to deliver and collect any balance due. He was able to maintain a pretty decent lifestyle working just three months each year. This is also the time to think about business Christmas cards, executive gifts, fruit and cheese baskets, etc.

Advertising Specialty Institute (ASI) – www.asicentral.com. Membership required.

Cost varies depending upon services subscribed to. Expensive and probably should not be considered until your volume in promotional products is substantial.

The truth is, most companies will not ask you for an ASI number. If someone does and you cannot overcome it, move on to the next company as they mostly sell the same types of stuff – or ask your printer friend (who you trust) if you can submit an order under his account as long as you pay a deposit, COD, etc.

TYPESETTERS & GRAPHIC DESIGNERS

Finding a typesetter and/or graphic artist

You will need someone to do your typesetting for the basic and graphic artists for the higher end work. Sometimes the two will overlap and a qualified artist will also handle the simple jobs from you in order to keep you happy.

Here is a general rule of thumb. If you are recreating a simple form for a customer, even if it has simple graphics in it – a typesetter is for you.

These would include:

- Letterheads
- Envelopes
- Forms
- Most of the simple, general things that don't have a "wow" factor

An artist might be for you if you are recreating or designing:

- A nice brochure
- Presentation folder
- Direct Mail Pieces
- Placement Ads in a magazine, etc.
- Anything with a design that was clearly not created by the person who set the address on the envelopes

There will be a sizeable difference in the amounts they charge as well.

I don't recommend doing the typesetting or artwork yourself *even if you know how*!

The only exception to this is if you are already a typesetter or graphic artist, you know what you're doing and, in most cases, would not be happy about paying someone else to do it.

A word of caution though – sometimes it's better to give the "grunt" work to someone who charges/earns less per hour than you do or would like to.

NOTE: Unless you get the original artwork from the customer, (very common) be sure that the art is all original and/or that they have specific license (permission) to use/sell any and all images used in the creation of your (on behalf of your customer) product. If not you may have to buy the license and bill the customer. This is usually only an issue for large national direct mailings, advertisements that will run in national publications and so on. It's extremely rare you will find it to be an issue on a local level even if your customer has customers all over the country.

How to find a typesetter or graphic artist

The easiest way is to use a classified service like Craigslist to locate someone in your area who does typesetting (typesetter) and also for someone who does graphic design work (graphic designer).

After you're in business a short while, you will start to see there are print designers and typesetters everywhere. There are many who work full time and would be very happy to work for you after hours.

NOTE: Be sure that they design for print. There are many "web designers" out there who feel there is no difference but if they are not experienced with designing for printing YOU will experience delays, printing issues (mistakes) that you have to pay for, delays and possibly the loss of your customer.

You can also outsource your typesetting and design to people you may find on Elance.com and Odesk.com.

You can build a great relationship with typesetters and designers there from all over the world. Just beware of the differences in time zones and cultural differences.

There are countless others but these are among some of the best. Be sure that the art is all original and/or that they have specific license (permission) to use/sell any and all images used in the creation of your product

TIP: Put a code word in it and tell them to make it the first word of their subject line. I use "soda".

This will weed out the people who just reply to everything. Bury it in there good in the product description.

Also - think about the product description:

It shouldn't be:

Typesetter wanted.

It should be more like:

Typesetter wanted for busy printing business to do a variety of ongoing typesetting work. Reply with the word soda in the subject line and provide a link to your portfolio.

You can also have logos created for customers and much more all at reasonable prices.

Proofing

A proof is a sample of the copy (text) and any artwork that may be getting ready for print. In it, you are making sure that all of the text and artwork is accurate and that nothing "shifted" in the design process.

A proof can be as simple as a PDF emailed to you, a print out from your desktop printer to more elaborate PMS color match proofs that will give an accurate representation of the final job when it's printed.

If the vendor emails you a proof DO NOT simply forward the proof along, it will have all of your vendors info in their signature. This is not how we want the customer to see us. Save the item, usually a PDF, to a folder on your computer or in the cloud then create a new email and attach it.

Keep in mind, usually one "PDF" proof is included, if you need a color matched proof, you will have to pay for it as well as shipping. Your customer will not want to wait a week to receive a proof from their "local" printer (you) so you will have to use an overnight service. These can be pricey and add up quickly.

Be sure to mention if there is a proof included in the price and the price of additional proofs.

This is where you can lose thousands if you're not careful. Earlier I mentioned an excellent trade printer DFS whose policy is to reprint whether or not it was their fault. That's great for you if you're printing with them exclusively but not good for you otherwise. In fact, even if they will rerun your jobs, your customers still needs them as promised.

So whose job is it to "proof" the material?

Technically, proofing falls solely on the shoulders of the customer. They provided you with the copy or sample and it is their job to check it.

In all likelihood even when they "miss" a typo, you may be blamed for it. They do not have the time and patience to review every letter of each word and make sure it's correct. Don't get me wrong one or two will but the majority will not.

You have to proof it. Let's face it, **you** are sending out the type/design to **your** designer therefore it makes sense that you read every word. Designers make errors just like anyone else. They are also likely to miss their typos just the same.

Even if you find a designer/typesetter who reads and reviews what they have done and tells you they have found a few errors, you still need to read it. Soon you will become very good at spotting them and will see them everywhere.

When you find an error *after your customer has "proofed"* it, you look like a hero who has **their** best interests in mind. Each time I spot an error, one customer or another reminds me of the many times I have "saved their butts." That's not a bad way to be remembered and builds loyalty.

A word of caution: Most people are decent and understand that they are selling you their product for at a set price with the full knowledge that you will be selling it for a profit. Some people will be unhappy to hear how much you are selling their printing (your printing) for if it is out of line with what *they think* it should be. Be careful about sharing with your vendor what you're selling price is to the end user – *your customer*. It's none of their business.

QUICK START GUIDE TO FINDING CUSTOMERS AND GETTING PAID FAST

Ok, this goes against everything I talked about in the chapter "You need customers".

I want you to understand how important it is to run your business and not let your business run you.

BUT

It's possible you need to make money today. You may be at the point where even a little amount of money will make a HUGE difference in your life ***this week***.

The material here is intended for just that. What I'm about to show you can be used every day for the rest of your business life but I don't recommend it. By using this method only your business will own you. You've been warned.

Selling to New Businesses

As I mentioned earlier, you may find people hunting for business cards at the office supply store.

These are usually new businesses that need some sort of printing. These are excellent sources of fast revenue. The type that will give you a deposit and pay COD because they are brand new and they don't expect or ask otherwise.

These are the easiest prospects to find and sell to as they are brand new, need some printing and usually don't have a clue where to begin.

They need:

- Business Cards
- Letterheads

- Envelopes
- Brochures
- Design work for all of these items

They don't spend a tremendous amount, but they spend enough to get you through the week in many cases and they are very excited to see their "dream business" in print. And you can easily get more than one new start-up customer per day.

As an added bonus, these customers are the easiest to reach by phone as they usually answer it themselves and are not in any position to critique your phone/cold calling skills. I.E. – not only do they provide fast pay, they provide excellent practice for your long term phone skills.

New businesses can be very strapped for cash. The easier you make it for them to pay the better. It's unlikely you have a current merchant account, but you can always accept payment via PayPal.

They can also pay you using PayPal COD using their card reader while you wait for them to complete the transaction. If you've never used PayPal before, it can take up to a day or two (or more if they mail you a check) to get paid, still, it's worth it the trouble. Visit PrintBrokerBook.com/resources for more information.

A better way (& one of my favorite ways) to find new businesses is:

- Look for them in the business section of the newspaper. Either in the "business" section or sometimes the classified advertisements.
- Be aware of press releases and other notifications in the press. (Note: These start-ups are more savvy and better funded. They may be harder to reach and get paid today!)

- Infofree.com – they provide, among other things, new business listing leads.

Here are some small businesses categories to help get you started:

- Small professionals such as accountants, insurance agencies and lawyers.
- Your local place of worship, association, group or favorite (local) charity. These groups are always in need of printing. They will harass you for the lowest price but you can still do ok with them if you need to get paid immediately.
- Retailers – Places that may use a lot of inexpensive flyers (like a window tinting shop) or higher end stores like boutiques and jewelers who will want to use "higher-end" printing to impress their customers and prove they belong.

Did you notice that I just gave you some powerful verbiage to use when speaking with these business owners?

Now, given that 95% of all new businesses fail, I do not recommend this method for the long haul.

Yes, some of these customers may become incredibly profitable but the odds are against that. And it may not serve you to bring them along while they struggle to climb their ladder to success.

As I stated before, your goal should be to get to the best customers as quickly as possible in order to build your business so you can live a great life.

NOTE: Always get a 50% deposit from a start-up. Even if they are your friend or family member, you want to be sure they have some "skin in the game."

GOAL SETTING & ACTION PLAN

Printers (and all people in any business) who set goals will be far more successful than those who do not.

In the beginning when I was struggling, I was unfocused and unorganized. It wasn't until I sat down and planned what I wanted my business to look like and find my reason "why" that enabled me to get things right.

Remember, my reason "why" wasn't just to "make money", even though that was why I started the business when I couldn't get a job, *it was to make a specific amount of money.* In my case, I needed $10,000. in order to buy my rent-to-own townhouse.

What is your reason why?

The first step is for you to set goals

If you already have goals, great. Congratulations. Work hard every day to meet those goals.

If not, you need to create some. You can have grandiose dreams like building your business to 10 million dollars a year but you are going to need to start somewhere and build up to that 10 million dollar a year business.

Think of it like a staircase. Each step takes you to the next one. Here's a sample:

- Step 1: Get legal – decide on your business entity and how you will collect payments.
- Step 2: Get your own printing

- Step 3: Tell your friends and family you started a business and ask them if they know anyone who needs printing.
- Step 4: Implement quick start guide
- Step 5: Get a customer
- Step 6: Get another customer
- Step 7: Repeat steps 5 & 6 over and over again
- Step 8: Reward yourself in some way (big or small)

Action Steps

Next, get out a calendar and put a customer and earnings goal for your first four weeks.

Then on the next month do it again. After that, go through the rest of the calendar make monthly goals of income and earnings.

Look at these goals daily. When you start your day think about what needs to be done to achieve those goals then do only those things.

As I mentioned earlier - stay off the internet. The internet is usually a place where productivity dies.

Don't let that happen to you.

The Truth About Social Media

A note on Social Media

Now I know this is not going to be very popular. But if you want to have a successful business you need to avoid the social media trap.

I said it - Social Media is a *TRAP*!

I know, most people love it, maybe you love it too. But as I've said before the internet (especially when using social media) is where productivity goes to die!

Will Facebook make you a millionaire overnight? You probably already know the answer to that.

Posting on your friends wall will, for 99.99% of us, yield nothing! That and hanging out with your "friends" all day makes you less productive.

The thing about all media as a marketing tool for our businesses is - Is it measurable?

Social media is just that – it is media. It is difficult to measure and quantify our efforts when using it to gain new business.

For our purposes it needs to be effective if we intend on using it. How will we know if it's effective?

The results can be measured like with direct mail.

With direct mail, if you mail 100 postcards and you get 2 customers you can determine what the mailing costs, the profit is now and for the life of the customer. A 2% return is industry standard – it can be much higher (or lower).

Ask youself if you can truly determine, like you can with direct mail, how much you will get back after you spend X amount of dollars. What is the return on investment?

If you can't answer that stick with some of the other methods.

I mention using Google Adwords and it can be effective. However, if you go that route, I encourage you to study it long and hard before you squander hundreds or thousands of dollars with nothing to show for it.

The traditional methods work best for printing. Keep in mind, we're not trying to become internet giants and you don't want to get bogged down with the customer service issues that come from people looking for their $10. set of business cards that you profited $2. on.

Think about this: Google spends millions of dollars marketing to business . . . ***using direct mail.***

They are mailing out $100. coupons to almost every business in the country for the sole purpose of getting them to buy advertising online.

And it's working.

Google is using the most effective form of marketing in the history of the universe to increase their market share.

I urge you to do the same.

Please be aware of the "Shiny Object Syndrome" where the next new shiny thing is what will draw your attention away from this, your business.

Stay focused.

CONCLUSION

I hope by now I have proven to you that you can do this.

With little start-up costs, no expensive equipment to buy and huge profits from repeat business print brokering as a business ranks right at the top.

That, and it provides a ton of freedom.

It might just change your life.

It did mine.

Change is scary and can sometimes be difficult. There may be people around you telling you that you can't do this, will not succeed, will fail.

Ignore them!

They will get over it, they always do.

I tell people to think of it like when you're driving on the highway about to pass someone driving slowly when suddenly

- THEY SPEED UP!

The don't speed up because they have just looked at the time, realized they were late and hit the gas.

Seeing you about to pass triggers a primal urge in them, it's an instinct. But then, after you pass them, they resume their normal speed, you look back in your rear-view and wonder, for moment, what that was about and then it's forgotten.

The people in your life are the same way.

They will adapt and come to appreciate your success even

though they (may have) seemed like they were trying to sabotage you.

Keep your head up, stay focused and follow the action plan provided next.

This is everything you need to get started. It is not everything you will ever need to know.

Naturally, in every field there are advanced techniques that require more training than can be discussed here, but you have everything you need to start your business immediately and be successful quickly.

Now **GO!**

Get started right now.

Be sure to visit the website for this book for book only bonuses and valuable resources.

PrintBrokerBook.com/resources

PrintBrokerBook.com/bonuses

I wish you the best of luck.

Brett

APPENDIX

Notes About Paper And Some Common Paper Sizes

Here is a small list of most of the paper sizes you will come across in the U.S. and most of the world. Not all sizes are noted.

US

- Letter (8 ½ x 11)
- Legal (8 ½ x 14)
- Tabloid (Ledger) (11 x 17)
- 13 x 19 inches
- 17 x 22 inches
- 22 x 34 inches
- 34 x 44 inches

Most of the world

- A5 (148 x 210 mm)
- A4 (210 x 297 mm)
- A3 (297 x 420 mm)
- A3+ (329 x 483 mm)
- A2 (420 x 594 mm)
- A1 (594 x 841 mm)
- A0 (841 x 1189 mm)

Paper is classified in type and weights (thicknesses). For instance regular copy paper is 20# (pound) weight but also comes in 24, 28, & 32, etc.

Almost all paper stocks come in different weights and will not be referenced individually here.

Just be aware of that fact when you are examining a stock you are trying to match.

- Bond (20#) – regular copy/printer paper
- Offset/Heavier (Bond) – same just a little thicker
- Laid
- Linen
- Opaque
- Enamel

Carbonless – a.k.a. – NCR

This is the type of paper that many contracts are written on. When you write on the top page, it transfers what you write to the other attached copies.

It comes in:

- 2-part
- 3 part
- 4-part, etc.
- Straight and Reverse (one is regular one-sided – the other is for double sided carbonless contracts such as initials)

If you absolutely have to match a paper stock, you can locate a local paper distributor, go to their storefront location (there are some in every major area) and they can help you.

Also, your local printer and designer friends can help as they probably have paper books and swatches you can compare against. You may even be able to borrow them to help your customer choose.

Glossary of Printing and Graphic Terms

I recommend reading and understanding these terms. The more essential terms are highlighted. Knowing these will help you be able to communicate better with your customers and vendors.

***Adhesive binding:** (see also Perfect Binding & PUR Binding) Type of thread-less binding in which the leaves of a book are held together at the binding edge by glue or synthetic adhesive.

Against the Grain: Folding at right angles to the grain direction of the paper being used, as opposed to with the grain. Also called across the grain and cross-grain. This can cause cracking on heavier papers unless the paper is scored or creased

Author's Corrections: Corrections made by the author on proofs, that alter the original copy. Author's corrections are chargeable at the discretion of the printer.

***Aqueous (coating)** – See varnish.

***Back Up:** Printing on the reverse side of a sheet already printed on one side. Back up position is critical and must be accurate to ensure consistent position throughout a folded product.

Bimetallic Plate: Plate in lithography used for long runs. The printing image base is usually copper and the non printing area is aluminum or stainless steel, giving a harder wearing plate than the conventional aluminum litho plate.

Black and White: Originals or reproductions in single color, also known as monotone or mono.

***Blanket:** In offset printing, a rubber surfaced fabric that is clamped around a plate cylinder to transfer the image from the impression cylinder to the substrate.

***Bleed:** When the printed image extends beyond the trimmed area of a page, the image must be increased. This extended area is known as the bleed.

Blind Embossing: The process of stamping an image into the paper to produce a depressed effect on the paper surface, without the use of inks.

***Blind Blocked:** In binding, to impress or stamp a design upon the cover. The design can be blocked in colored inks, or metal foil, including special effects such as holographic.

Bond Paper: A grade of writing or printing paper, usually used for letterheads or business forms.

BPOP: Abbreviation for “Bulk packed onto pallets”.

Broadsheet: Any sheet in its basic size (not folded or cut); also denotes a newspaper format.

***Camera Ready:** Artwork or copy ready for photographic reproduction.

Case: In bookbinding, the hard covers of a case bound book

Chalking: When the dry ink on a printed piece can be rubbed off. Happens when there is insufficient bond between the pigment and the vehicle.

Chill Marking: Marking caused by the chill rollers on a heatset web press, which cool the web after drying.

Chromolithography: Color printing by means of lithography.

***CMYK:** **C**yan, **M**agenta, **Y**ellow, Blac**K** (**K**ey), being the primary colors used as the basis for 4-color process printing. Also known as 4 color process.

***Coated Stock:** Material coated on one or both sides with a mixture china clay, latex and other loadings to fill up surface pits and improve the printing surface. a.k.a. C1S – C2S

Cockling: Deformation of a sheet of paper due to unequal shrinkage giving it a slightly crumpled appearance.

Coldset Web: A reel fed press with limited or no drying facility.
Only uncoated papers such as newsprint or bond can be printed on coldset webs.

***Color Correction:** Alteration of the color of a photographic image by electronic retouching.

***Color Proofing:** This term describes a wide range of techniques which have been developed to reproduce full color images from film or digital data available, prior to the actual print run; thus allowing the customer and printer to view the "proofed" result, prior to the actual print run.

***Color Separation:** In photographic reproduction, the process of separating color originals into the primary printing color components.

Concertina Fold: Folding each panel of a leaflet in alternate directions, so that when opened out the finished product is folded in a zigzag fashion.

Contact Print: A photographic print made from a negative or positive in contact with sensitised paper, film or printing plate.

Continuous Tone: A photographic image with gradient

tones from black to white.

Contrast: The tonal gradation between the highlights, middle tone and shadows in an original or reproduction.

Crease: An indented line pressed into the substrate to reduce resistance and allow folding without cracking or splitting.

***Crop:** To cut a piece of copy or artwork to the size indicated on an original by cropmarks.

***Crop Marks:** In printing, marks placed on the copy to indicate where the paper should be trimmed.

Crossover: When an image runs across two pages, requiring the image to be split where it crosses the spine.

***CTP:** Acronym for Computer To Plate, the process by which digital data is converted via a RIP device to drive a platesetter, which generates the finished printing plate.

Curl: In paper, the distortion of a sheet due to differences in structure or coatings from one side to the other or absorption of moisture on an offset press.

Cut-Off: In web offset printing, the cut length of a single revolution of the printing cylinder. Conventional long grain presses have a 620 to 630mm cut-off, whereas short grain presses typically have 560 to 600mm cut-off.

Deckle Edge: The untrimmed ragged edges of paper formed at the outer edge of a jumbo reel of paper on a papermaking machine.

***Densitometer:** A device for measuring the color density at a specific location on film or printed product, either by reflected or transmitted light.

***Die-Cutting:** The process of using sharp steel blades known as rules to cut a shape into paper or board.

***Die-stamping:** An intaglio process of printing in which the resultant impression stands out in relief above the surface of the stamped material, either colored (using inks or foil) or blind (no inks or foils).

***Digital Color Proofs:** A color proof produced from digital data. Digital proofs may be Pre-RIP (before rendering pixels), or Post-RIP. Low resolution proofs are generally used to check content only and High resolution to check color matching.

Dithering: A technique of filling the gap between two pixels with another pixel having an average value of the two to smooth out the resulting image.

***Dot:** The individual element in both halftones and four color process printing.

***Dot Gain:** In printing, a defect in which dots print larger than they should, causing darker tones and stronger colors.

***Dots Per Inch:** (dpi) A measure of resolution on the printed page.

Drawn-on Cover: A paper book cover, which is attached to the sewn book by gluing the spine.

Drop-Out: Fine halftone dots or fine lines which are eliminated from the highlight areas of the plate during the plate making process.

Duotone: A two-color halftone reproduction from a one color photograph.

***Dummy:** A sample of a proposed job made up with the actual materials and cut to the correct size to show bulk, style of binding etc. Also a complete layout of a job showing position of type matter and illustrations, margins etc.

Duplex Paper: A paper with a different color or finish on either side of the sheet

***Embossing:** The process of impressing an image in relief into the paper to produce a raised effect on the paper surface, without the use of inks.

Emulsion Side: The side of the film coated with a light-sensitive emulsion.

***EPS:** Encapsulated Post Script, a computer file format usually used to transfer post script information from one book to another.

Filmsetter: An output device which produces film positives or negatives directly from Ripped data.

Fit: Printers' terminology for the accurate positioning of all of the elements of one color with all of the elements of another color on a printed sheet. Sheets may "register" but not fit.

Flexography: A relief process in which printing is done from a rubber or plastic stereo (plate). Flexo presses can print on a wide variety of substrates including metal and plastic, but print quality is inferior to litho or gravure.

Folio: The page number.

Form: In printing, one side of assembled pages or other images for printing. In die-cutting, the wooden board in which the cutting, creasing and perforating rules are mounted.

***Four-color Process:** Technique of printing that uses black, magenta, cyan and yellow to simulate full-color images. Colors are reproduced by combinations of these four process colors. Also called process printing.

***FPO:** An acronym (For Position Only) used in mechanical presentation to identify the crop specifications on a specific piece of composition.

Galley Proof: A proof of text before being made up into pages. Also known as a slip proof.

***Ganging-up (Gang-run or running):** Imposing different images on a sheet to save make-readies. Different ratios of images can be used to create different quantities; for instance a sheet 8 images can be printed 4: 3: 1, so each 1,000 printed sheets would contain 4,000 of image one, 3,000 of image two and 1,000 of image three.

Ghosting: Phenomenon of a faint image appearing on a printed sheet where it was not intended to appear.

Gilding: In book printing, the application of gold leaf to the edges of a book.

***Grain:** The direction in which most of the fibres run. Tear any piece of paper and it will have one direction where it tears in a straight line (the grain direction) and one where the tear is more ragged (across the grain). Wetting a strip paper will cause it to curl in the opposite direction to the grain.

Gravure: Printing process in which recesses on a printing cylinder are filled with ink and the surplus removed by a doctor blade. The paper contacts the cylinder and 'lifts' the ink from the recesses, creating a much heavier ink film than lithography.

Grey Balance: The combination of the four process colors which produce a neutral grey.

Grind-Off: The area which runs along the spine of each section (signature) of a perfect bound book which is removed after being gathered to allow the glue to penetrate every leaf.

***Gutter:** The blank space or inner margin from printing area to binding.

***Halftone:** The reproduction of continuous-tone artwork into a series of dots.

Hickeys: In offset lithography, spots or imperfection in the printing due to contamination on the press, such as paper particles, dried ink spots etc.

***Impression:** In printing, the pressure of the plate or blanket as it comes in contact with paper.

***Imposition:** Arrangement of pages in a sequence, which will read consecutively when the printed sheet is folded.

Intaglio: Printing method in which the image in the plate is etched or recessed. The ink is applied to the plate, wiped clean and then the ink remaining in the recesses transfers to the substrate.

***Jog:** To align sheets of paper into a pile prior to cutting.

Kiss-Cut: Light cut into the peelable surface of a self adhesive sheet, leaving the backing sheet intact.

Laid: Finish on bond or text paper on which grids of parallel lines simulate the surface of handmade paper.

***Lamination:** A plastic film bonded by heat and pressure to a printed sheet.

Landscape: Orientation of the sheet or end-product where the horizontal dimension is greater than the vertical.

***Letterpress:** Method of printing from raised surfaces, either metal type or plates whose surfaces have been etched away from image areas. Also called block printing.

Limp Cover: A flexible book cover, as distinct from a cased-in board cover.

Line Copy: Copy suitable for reproduction without using a halftone screen.

Lithographic (Litho) printing: Method of printing using plates whose image areas attract ink and whose non-image areas repel ink. Non-image areas may be coated with water to repel the oily ink or may have a surface, such as silicon, that repels ink.

Long grain press: A press where the longest side of the standard folded product runs parallel to the grain of the paper.

***Loose Insert:** Any item inserted into a printed product without being affixed in any way.

Machine finished (MF): Any finish obtained on a papermaking machine.

***Make-Ready:** In printing, all work done to set up a press for printing, before impression count is activated and good copies are produced.

Mechanical: A term for a camera-ready paste-up of artwork.

Mid Tones: The tonal range between highlights and shadows of a photograph or reproduction.

*__Moiré:__ Screen pattern caused by a clash of screen angles in litho reproduction.

Mottle: The bruised or spotted appearance of the printed image.

Mylar: A stable polyester film used as a base for film mounting or a grid for mounting perforating and scoring rules.

Nipping: In the book binding process, a stage where air is expelled from its contents at the sewing stage.

*__Offset:__ In printing, the process of using an intermediate blanket cylinder to transfer an image from the impression cylinder to the substrate.

Outsert: A printed element which is usually stitched to the outside of a magazine cover.

Overprinting: Printing onto a sheet which has been previously printed. Typically used to add dealer addresses to generic brochures.

*__Pantone (PMS):__ The Pantone Matching System (PMS) is a color standard which defines a wide range of color solids and the combination of process colors required to achieve the closest match to the solid Pantone color.

*__PDF (Portable Digital Format):__ PDF is a multi-platform file format developed by Adobe Systems. A PDF file captures document text, fonts, images, and even formatting of documents from a variety of applications.

*__Perfect Binding:__ A method of adhesive binding with a square-backed spine. Individual sections are collected together and the spine is ground off. Hot-melt glue is then applied to the spine and a cover drawn on before the product is trimmed flush to the final size.

Perfecting Press: A printing press that prints both sides of the sheet in one pass through the press.

***Pica:** A unit of measure in the printing industry. A pica is approximately 0.166 in. There are 12 points to a pica.

Pick-up Page: An exact repeat of a page used in a previous edition.

Pin Marks: In web printing, the web of paper can be driven into the folder by pins which penetrate the surface the web on the outer edges of the sheet. The resulting holes are called pin marks. Pin marks are usually trimmed off but newspapers often have visible pin marks.

Pin Register: The use of datum points punched into copy, film and plates to ensure that the color separation is accurate.

***Pixel:** In electronic imaging, the basic unit of digital imaging.

Plate Cylinder: The cylinder of a press onto which the printing plate is mounted.

Platesetter: An output device which produces a finished printing plate directly from Ripped data. Also known as a CTP device.

***Point:** The size of the font. This is an example of 12 point (pt) type.

***Portrait:** Orientation of a sheet or end-product where the vertical dimension is greater than the horizontal.

***PostScript:** A page description language (PDL) developed by Adobe, which defines the contents and layout of a page in electronic form. PostScript is also bookming language which is interpreted by a PostScript RIP in output devices such as film setters or plate setters (CTP) in order to reproduce the original page.

*Pre-Press: The stage of the print production process which takes place after design and before printing.

Primary Colors: Additive and subtractive primary colors can be mixed to form all other colors. The additive primary colors are red, green and blue (RGB) and can be added together to make all other colors, as is done when light is emitted from the screen of a television set or computer monitor. The subtractive primary colors (cyan, magenta and yellow) are those that, when mixed, subtract light from white to make all the other colors. This is what happens when pigments are mixed to create printing inks.

*Process Printing: Printing using the process color set (CMYK).

*Proof: A representation of the printed product which is checked prior to print production.

PUR Binding: The same process as perfect binding, but a synthetic adhesive(Polyurethane React) is used in place of conventional hot-melt glue. The glued spine is more pliable and the adhesive bond much stronger than a perfect bound product and so has increased longevity.

Quarter-fold: Two or more folds, each fold at 90 degrees to the previous one. Also called right-angle fold.

Ream: Five hundred sheets of paper.

Register: Adjustment of color plates to obtain perfect super imposition of colors.

Register Marks: Cross-hair lines on mechanicals, films and plates used for positioning pages or images to enable accurate register on press.

RGB: Red, green, blue additive primary colors. RGB files must be converted to CMYK at the pre-press stage prior to printing 4 color process.

***Rich Black:** an ink mixture of solid black over one or more of the other CMYK colors, resulting in a darker tone than black ink alone generates in a 4 color printing process. Black on its own may appear dull, faded or washed out. Creating text in rich black enhances the color and tone, making it a truer representation of the intended artwork.

***RIP:** Acronym for Raster Image Processor, which generates a bitmap to send to the printing device (film setter, platesetter or digital press). The input data is either a file written in a page description language such as PDF or another bitmap. In the latter case, the RIP applies either smoothing or interpolation algorithms to the input bitmap to generate the output bitmap.

Rotary Trimmed: In-line trimming of a product as it passes over slitting knives. Very cost effective, but can leave a "feathered" edge.

Run-Around: In composition, type set to fit around a picture or other design element.

Saddle-stitch: Method of binding where folded sections are inset and secured together with wire staples (also known as wire-stitch).

Safelight: Lamp used for illumination of a darkroom without affecting light-sensitive materials.

***Scanner:** An electronic device used to convert a

continuous tone original into a series of halftone dots for printing.

***Score:** To impress or indent a mark with a string or rule in the paper, to make folding easier.

***Self-Cover:** Using the same paper as the text as a cover. Usually done with heavier weight stocks such as enamel.

***Serif/Sans Serif:** The short cross-strokes at the ends of the main strokes of letters in some typefaces. Fonts with these cross-strokes are known as serif faces and those without are known as sans serif.

***Set Off:** Transfer of ink from one printed sheet to another.

Short grain press: A press where the shortest side of the finished product runs parallel to the grain of the paper.

Show through: The degree to which a printed image is visible through the paper due to the lack of opacity of the paper.

Signature: In printing and binding, a printed sheet after it has been folded. Also called a section.

Slurring: In litho printing, the dragging of the wet ink which causes the dots to elongate in the direction the press travel.

Spine glued: A product which is held together with a thin film of adhesive running down the spine of each page. Can be produced in-line on some web presses.

Spiral Binding: A book bound with wires in spiral form inserted through holes punched along the binding.

***Spot varnish:** The application of varnish to selective

areas to create a highlight or contrast effect.

***Step-and-Repeat:** The multiple exposure of an image by stepping it in multiple positions and exposing in each position to create a repeat pattern using one original image.

Stock: Most commonly used as the term for the paper type used in a printed job.

Substrate: The piece of material printed (e.g. paper, board, plastic, tin).

Tack: That property, governed by viscosity and adhesion, which renders a film of printing ink sticky to the touch.

Tint: Screening or adding white to a solid color in order to lighten that specific color. In lithography, the tint is achieved by creating dots to reduce the strength of the solid color.

Tolerances: The specification of acceptable variations in a range of printing parameters to take account of the imperfections in each process.

Trapping: To print a wet ink film over previously printed ink.
Dry trapping is printing wet ink or varnish over dry ink. Wet trapping is printing wet ink or varnish over previously printed wet ink.

***Trim Marks:** In printing, marks placed on the copy to indicate where the paper should be trimmed.

Undercolor Removal: Technique of making color separations such that the amount of cyan, magenta and yellow ink is reduced in shadow areas while the amount of black is increased. Abbreviated UCR.

***Up:** In printing, the number-“Up” is the number of unique images on the printed sheet i.e. a 5 ½ x 8 ½ postcard fits 2- - up on an 8 ½ x 11 sheet

***UV Varnish:** A liquid coating applied to a printed sheet for protection and enhancement, which is dried immediately by exposure to UV light.

***Varnishing:** The application of any form of liquid varnish to printed matter in order to enhance its appearance or increase its durability.

Vignette: A design or illustration in which the background fades gradually away to white.

Viscosity: The amount of tack and flow of a printing ink or varnish.

***Web:** The roll of paper used in web or rotary printing. Also a term for a web printing press.

***Web Offset:** The offset printing process on a press which prints on a roll or web of paper.

***Web Press:** A press which prints on a roll or web of paper.

Wire-o Binding: A continuous double series of wire loops run through punched slots along the binding side of a booklet.

Wire Side: Side of the paper that rests against the manufacturing wires during papermaking. Typically the rougher side of the paper.

With the Grain: Parallel to the grain direction of the fibres of the paper or board, as opposed to against the grain.

Woodfree: Paper with no mechanical wood pulp. Woodfree papers actually contain wood pulp which has been chemically treated to enhance the whiteness of the paper.

***Work and Tumble:** In sheet fed printing, to print one side of a sheet paper, then turn it over from grip edge to back (leave) edge, using the same plate and side lay to print the second side but using a different grip edge.

***Work and Turn:** In sheet fed printing, to print one side of a sheet paper, then turn it over from left to right and print the second side using the same grip and plate but opposite side lay.

Made in the USA
Middletown, DE
16 March 2015